Praise for *Enablement Mastery*

"Elay Cohen, one of the greatest minds in sales enablement, has captured a vast amount of knowledge from his experience over the years to give us the what, the why, and the how of this exciting industry. *Enablement Mastery* shares the pros and cons as well as the highs and lows of Elay's journey as a sales enablement leader. Cohen also provides valuable ideas and game plans to help others on their journey. It's rare you find a book that will be a reference for the future. This book has valuable insights and ideas on every page. A home run!"

—Howard Dover, Ph.D.; Director, Center for Professional Sales, Naveen Jindal School of Management, University of Texas at Dallas

"Elay is hands down the best enablement leader I've worked with over the years. *Enablement Mastery* is a proven playbook for CEOs and leadership teams to embrace if you want to transform culture by aligning and enabling teams to scale. Well done, Elay!"

—Rob Acker, CEO, Salesforce.org

"Elay Cohen is a legend in the sales enablement industry, and I wholeheartedly endorse *Enablement Mastery*. Anyone starting, or looking to improve, their sales learning function needs to read this book first."

—Brian Frank, Vice President, Global Sales Operations, LinkedIn

"*Enablement Mastery* is awesome. As a CFO, enablement as a percentage of revenue is something I think about a lot and I believe every C-suite member should be an evangelist of enablement. *Enablement Mastery* is a great roadmap for companies to tie enablement strategies with company strategies versus being an afterthought."

—**Elena Gomez,** Chief Financial Officer, Zendesk

"Elay has cracked the code on sales success for large hyper-growth companies. Elay's success as the former SVP of Sales Productivity at Salesforce and decades of experience working with some of the fastest growing technology companies make him the expert in the industry, as shown in *Enablement Mastery*. This book is filled with strategies and practical advice to help leaders solve their top growth challenges."

—**Arjun Gupta,** Chief Believer, Telesoft;
Executive Chairman, SalesHood

"In 35 years of sales transformation projects, I have met only a few leaders who have helped generate billions of dollars of shareholder value and Elay was (and is) the thought leader by far. Elay's success is legendary. Elay goes beyond the theory of enablement and is able to create repeatable, predictable, and measurable selling results. *Enablement Mastery* is *the* book for creating great enablement leaders and highly functioning enablement teams."

—**Barry Rhein,** Founder, Selling Through Curiosity

"*Enablement Mastery* is more than a book about sales enablement, it is a workbook that helps a practitioner at any stage of their career take their sales enablement effect to the next level. Whether you are just getting started, or have been in your role for a while, you'll take away expert insight and guidance that can be implemented immediately."

—**Carol Sustala,** Vice President, Sales Enablement
PowerSchool Group

"With *Enablement Mastery*, Elay Cohen enabled us with a masterpiece on sales enablement! A captivating roadmap to help shape your vision for sales enablement, this book also helps you blend the right enablement culture, organizational design, and process for a successful go-to-market strategy. A must-read for any leaders in sales, marketing, and learning and development roles in modern organizations."

—**Joël Le Bon,** Ph.D.; Professor, Sales and Marketing;
Director, Leadership in Digital Marketing and Transformation;
Carey Business School, John Hopkins University

"If you want to know how to make your organization achieve revenue excellence, shorten your learning curve and read *Enablement Mastery*. Elay's book is practical, proven, uniquely insightful, and based on experience and hard lessons from the trenches. It's the Holy Grail of enablement. Elay's book contains the schematic, now execute!"

—**Robert M. Peterson,** Ph.D.; Dean's Distinguished
Professor of Sales, NIU Professional Sales Program,
Northern Illinois State University

"Elay does the enablement profession a huge service by writing *Enablement Mastery*. His book is perfect for practitioners who want to systematically improve the performance of the entire sales force and impact massive growth. Moving from tactics and tools into the strategic value of the role is how we will elevate the enablement profession."

—**Scott Santucci,** Founder, Sales Enablement Society; President, Growth Enablement Ecosystems

"Elay's new book *Enablement Mastery* is very illuminating for sales enablement professionals. It should become their bible. Elay captured the emerging trends of learning, communicating, and collaborating using video. The book captures the amazing inside story at Salesforce, from Marc Benioff's vision, to execution of the sales enablement initiative. Elay humbly shares some of his own mistakes and realistic political battles that are inevitable on his journey to success. The book is real and authentic. Congratulations to Elay on an outstanding, insightful, practical, and inspiring book."

—**Gerhard Gschwandtner,** CEO, Selling Power

"If you are a professional sales leader or are a non-profit trying to have more meaningful conversations with your customers or donors, this book is for you."

—**Lynne Smith,** Vice President, Digital Services, United Way Worldwide

ENABLEMENT
MASTERY

ELAY COHEN

ENABLEMENT MASTERY

GROW YOUR BUSINESS FASTER BY ALIGNING YOUR PEOPLE, PROCESSES, AND PRIORITIES

GREENLEAF
BOOK GROUP PRESS

Published by Greenleaf Book Group Press
Austin, Texas
www.gbgpress.com

Distributed by Greenleaf Book Group

For ordering information or special discounts for bulk purchases, please contact Greenleaf Book Group at PO Box 91869, Austin, TX 78709, 512.891.6100.

Design and composition by Greenleaf Book Group
Cover design by Greenleaf Book Group

Cataloging-in-Publication data is available.

Print ISBN: 978-1-62634-574-4

eBook ISBN: 978-1-62634-575-1

Part of the Tree Neutral® program, which offsets the number of trees consumed in the production and printing of this book by taking proactive steps, such as planting trees in direct proportion to the number of trees used: www.treeneutral.com

Printed in the United States of America on acid-free paper

19 20 21 22 23   10 9 8 7 6 5 4 3 2

First Edition

Dearest Jenn (said the right way),
Thank you for everything you do for us.
P.S. I love you.

Contents

Foreword

Messaging is one of my top priorities as a chief revenue officer. When companies are growing at a very fast rate and you're creating a new category and educating the market, it's so critical to have everyone aligned around the same message as a company. Enablement to me is the way to drive that consistency to drive better performance, better attainment for our salespeople, and therefore drive up our revenue as a company, all while improving the retention rate of our sales team and limit the churn.

I started selling a long time ago. This is my fourth decade of selling. I started with IBM selling mainframe computers on Wall Street for many years. I ended up in Tokyo for a number of years with IBM running sales in Asia. IBM then moved me to Silicon Valley in the late nineties. I left IBM to go to Ariba, a hot internet startup in the early 2000s when the Internet bubble was just about to burst. From there I left to go to Salesforce where I was on an amazing rocket ship ride for over twelve years.

There is no other company like Salesforce that represented sales acceleration and sales excellence more than they did. Marc Benioff inspired us with his vision to change the world, to disrupt the industry, and to become the market leader.

Right after we went public at Salesforce we hired Elay

Cohen to help our sales messaging, sales playbook, and stories that were all over the map. We lacked consistency. What Marc Benioff was saying in his visionary "cloud" presentations and keynotes and what our salespeople were saying were completely different. We were against the entire software industry and It was so important that we had the messaging right and we had the stories right.

Elay brought passion, discipline and enthusiasm to the Salesforce culture. He inspired all of us to be the best we can be. We created sales playbooks and a winning sales success formula to get our teams selling the same way. We aligned everyone on a consistent message with training and certification. We were disciplined about it. Elay made sure of it. Everyone at all levels in the company had to practice their pitches quarter after quarter, year after year. We got the whole company aligned and on message with Marc Benioff's vision and messaging by being disciplined about how we coached and enabled our teams. The way Elay enabled our teams proved to change the trajectory of the company in an incredibly positive way. The strategy of getting teams aligned on messaging and coaching managers and individuals to rehearse and practice their pitches is a true competitive differentiator.

Enablement ultimately helped grow and move the company up and to the right. Focusing on sales readiness and skills development is so critical to helping increase sales productivity and time to ramp. Why wouldn't we want to always give our teams the right coaching and tools to help make all of them absolute A+ players?

Elay is a trusted resource and thought leader I've leaned on for many years. He was my go-to person at Salesforce when we were growing fast. He continues to be there for me and my teams, 24/7. I encourage every CEO, CRO and CMO to spend quality time with Elay. He is a revenue game-changer. Elay multiplies the effectiveness of any organization, and can help your enablement team truly become multipliers as well.

He will help you grow your business faster. He will teach you how to embrace enablement as a growth driver. Elay's new company SalesHood encapsulates the best of all of these experiences from Salesforce, making them available to millions of people. He's taking the best practices to every company with his company SalesHood.

Elay's new book *Enablement Mastery* captures years of best practices in a very well organized and thoughtful structure that can be easily applied to pretty much any organization.

His book is a great collection of tips, stories, and lessons learned, created to help leaders align their people, processes, and priorities. Organizational enablement never ends. You can't check the box and say we've completed enablement. It's always evolving. It's an iterative process. The enablement journey is key to every sales organization, but just as importantly the overall organization.

Enablement Mastery is an important resource and asset for every revenue leader and sales organization or CEO who wants to transform their organization on the planet.

Elay, congratulations on this great accomplishment.

—Jim Steele
President & Chief Revenue Officer,
Yext

Preface

Only a few people on the planet have the experience and expertise to help companies grow revenues tenfold under the banner of sales enablement. Imagine what it is like to energize, educate, and enable the sales teams responsible for the fastest growth story in technology history. That was my world from 2005 to 2013. I published my first book, *SalesHood: How Winning Sales Managers Inspire Sales Teams to Succeed*, about that experience. *SalesHood* is about helping companies and front-line managers build the right sales coaching culture and cadence.

Arthur Do and I also founded SalesHood, a software company focused on accelerating revenue and increasing sales productivity with a modern enablement platform. Our founding vision was to inspire people and companies to be the best they could be by sharing and spreading knowledge at scale. We wanted to take the enablement best practices and guiding principles that worked well at Salesforce and scale them using technology. Over a five-year period, working with tens of thousands of salespeople, we proved that enablement could be a revenue multiplier. Our Journey showed us how important enablement is to every CEO on the planet. We also realized that enablement is a company-wide initiative and not just a sales phenomenon. Universities and business schools started reaching out to us to learn more about the discipline of enablement too.

Given my experience in the industry, I decided to write a new book rich with practical knowledge and frameworks to serve as the foundation to improve corporate enablement strategies and develop people to execute the strategies. The goal of *Enablement Mastery* is to help every company and team grow faster by aligning its people, processes, and priorities.

Executive of the Year

In 2011, Marc Benioff recognized me as executive of the year. If you would have told me in my early teens that I would be recognized as an executive of the year by one of the most powerful technology CEOs on the planet, I wouldn't have believed you.

I remember sitting at the awards dinner in the Wynn Hotel conference room in Las Vegas with hundreds of the top executives from Salesforce and thousands of people who had tuned in via video conference. Marc got onstage and started recognizing executives for their leadership and results in their respective areas of the business. We celebrated the leaders who were achieving excellence. They were the ones who believed and made it happen. One by one each leader was brought up onstage and congratulated. Marc recognized the top product leader, top sales leader, top marketing leader, and top customer-success leader. I remember sitting at my table wondering if they even had a category for the work my team did. What would that category be? Then Marc got to the most prestigious award—the executive of the year. He started describing the person who would soon be recognized, explaining the effect this person had at the company. As he went on, the person started sounding familiar to me.

That's because it *was* me.

Marc called me up onstage to accept the recognition and the award. It was one of the highest points of my professional career and life. Years of work and dedication had gotten me to that point. At that moment, my life flashed in front of my eyes. I remembered selling furniture at my dad's furniture store. I could smell the grass from all the lawns I had cut during the summers when I had my own gardening and landscaping business. I remembered my time selling first aid supplies and learning how to cold call by knocking on doors in industrial parks in Toronto. I remembered helping clients and selling investments and loans at TD Canada Trust. I remembered my time as a product manager at a startup and then my time at Oracle. All these experiences led to this moment.

My story became clear. I am a doer who is motivated to help people be the best they can be.

I was recognized as executive of the year at Salesforce at the time that I was senior vice president of sales productivity. We had just completed a company-wide launch of new messaging and certifications around an initiative that was near and dear to the heart of our CEO. My team and I stepped up and ensured that every employee understood the importance of the new corporate pitch. We enabled a company-wide transformation by creating a curriculum that we rolled out to every sales and customer-facing employee in the company for training, coaching, assessment, and certification. They learned it and had fun doing it, too. We exceeded expectations.

As I reflect a few years later, I am still floored that a CEO recognized an operational leader for accomplishments in sales enablement. It was a nontraditional executive recognition. We proved that knowledge sharing and enablement is a top CEO priority. Enablement as a strategic imperative by a CEO would soon be a trend that would become much more common.

I asked my former boss, Linda Crawford, to share why she thought Marc and the executive committee decided to recognize the work we did at the time. She said: "Salesforce was in hypergrowth mode, and the company needed to recognize leaders and teams for helping to achieve its big goals with innovative multipliers. You did it and proved your knowledge-sharing process was a home run for the company."

I am excited when I see other CEOs recognize their executive team for successes in enablement and knowledge-sharing. Mostly, I believe they see how it contributes to revenue, leadership development, and culture.

Introduction

Enablement is most effective when it is company-wide, when it is top-down and bottom-up, starting with the CEO and touching every employee, partner, and customer. It is inclusive of all departments, teams, and roles. Everyone plays a part. Everyone is enabled.

There's a shortage of practical guides and business books written for companies to execute successful cross-company enablement. That's why I wrote this book. I'd like to give company leaders, managers, and individual contributors a process map to be the best they can by mastering enablement. The essence of enablement mastery is to help companies grow their business faster by aligning their people, processes, and priorities.

People

Mastering enablement starts with your people. The first part of this book answers the following about enablement professionals: who they are, how they found themselves in enablement jobs, what motivates them, their responsibilities, why they do what they do, where they fit inside an organizational structure, and whether they live in sales or marketing or human resources.

We must help enablement professionals earn their seat at the table by being better communicators and by finding the right balance of strategic thinking versus tactical execution. They need to know how to secure organizational buy-in for enablement initiatives. Since this role is new, it's important that enablement professionals are mindful about how their peers perceive their brand.

After reading the first section of this book, you'll know how to profile and hire the right enablement people, how to structure your enablement team, and how to set your organization up for success with the right enablement mindset. Enablement is a company-wide initiative, and I want to help you secure organizational buy-in top-down and bottom-up to ensure everyone is aligned.

Processes

With the right people and teams in place, we shift focus to the Enablement Process Map, which will become the common language to improve cross-departmental collaboration. Learn how to set teams up for success by working better together. Depending on how organizations are structured, different team members and departments will own different enablement processes. In some cases, marketing may own content development, and in other cases enablement managers may be the publishers. It's imperative that a process map exists that is agreed upon by all stakeholders. The processes cross teams and functions. They include go-to-market, learning, communications, customer engagement, and achievements.

After reading this section, you will have clarity around how to use the Enablement Process Map to facilitate better collaboration on cross-company initiatives. When teams come together to work on programs and initiatives, they will be able to use the Enablement Process Map to easily and efficiently sort out how work gets done and who owns what. Friction will be reduced with better alignment of people and processes.

Priorities

The final part of this book discusses specific challenging enablement priorities, but when executed by the right people following the right processes, you'll achieve great results. We'll tackle hard programs like enabling front-line managers, kicking off events, and building modern universities. These are considered priorities suited for mature organizations. For some, they will be mission critical, for others, aspirational.

Company-Wide Enablement Is a CEO Top Priority

Since we're professing the importance of company-wide enablement, let's review why you should care and what this means to the many different roles in a company.

CEOs will want enablement mastery to realize their company growth goals through company-wide alignment. Sales leaders will want enablement mastery to boost the distribution of sales attainment. Marketing leaders will subscribe to enablement mastery to more efficiently and effectively deliver relevant content to sales and the company. Human resource leaders will appreciate enablement mastery because they will gain a new appreciation of modern learning and reinvent their corporate contributions. Enablement leaders, both present and future, will better understand what it takes to align people, processes, and priorities inside the complex realities and politics of a company.

One of the goals in writing this book is to increase awareness and execution of successful enablement strategies and tactics by avoiding enablement that's considered bad and ineffective. The path to enablement mastery is not an easy one. An Enablement Process Map is required to help organizational leaders have constructive conversations about who owns what and how work gets done. My goal in this book is to empower you with all the tools to bring your enablement vision to life with a strategy that aligns people, processes, and priorities while incorporating organizational buy-in at all levels.

PART ONE

PEOPLE

Chapter 1

My Early Days in Enablement at Salesforce

When Marc Benioff invited me to attend executive meetings in his Salesforce office in San Francisco to discuss the latest corporate pitch presentation, he would assemble the heads of product marketing, corporate communications, and sales to join us. He would go through the presentation slide by slide and explain the rationale behind each. He would share customer examples. He would explain the story arc and the logic behind the presentation flow. He would highlight competitive land mines and emphasize Salesforce's unique differentiators. Everyone around the table took notes. Slides were updated in real time. The energy was engaging and tense. Everyone wanted to win. That was the culture. It was the ultimate in messaging alignment.

After spending a couple hours reviewing the presentation, Marc would turn to me and say, "Now it's your turn." He meant that we now had a new corporate presentation that he had blessed along with his marketing leaders, and he wanted it to be rolled out to sales and customer-facing employees. The rollout was my job. My team and I were responsible for training, coaching, and certifying our teams.

Marc would then specify the timeline, saying, "I want everyone *certified* on the latest corporate presentation within thirty days." He wanted every sales and customer-facing employee to practice and deliver the corporate pitch in front of a person who would sign off that they had delivered the presentation on message and according to expectations. That was what being certified on a corporate presentation meant. Marc knew how valuable this was to Salesforce's success and growth.

As a group, before we would leave Marc's office, we would negotiate the timeline and scope of the company-wide certification. We usually had thirty to sixty days to get everyone to confidently deliver the latest Salesforce corporate pitch presentation. We would then assemble the materials with coaching aids and roll them out to the global Salesforce teams. Sometimes we included partners. I was personally responsible to sit down with every president and vice president and certify them. We subscribed to the notion of leading by example, and managers always had to be certified first.

We experimented by trial and error to find what worked and what didn't in getting everyone properly certified. The first practice was to publish the pitch with speaker notes, maybe with video, and perhaps with support-office hours. After we certified every sales leader, my team and I would fly around the world and have reps present their pitch in local offices in order to get everyone certified. This process was highly inefficient and costly.

A second way we tried to get everyone certified was to have reps present their pitch back to their sales manager. When we did it this way, after a few slides, many sales managers would say, "You got it. Now let's look at your forecast." Many times, the pitch review would not be completed.

A third experiment we tried was to have individuals upload their certification pitches to a central file library. The result was that no one watched the pitches, which sat in a folder collecting digital dust. The bigger consequence of these scenarios is our teams missed the benefits of watching each other pitch.

We always got the certifications done. We had to. What we didn't execute so well was scaling the cross-team, cross-geo knowledge sharing we knew our sales teams wanted. We did this by flying people to a central location and having the top performers share their winning stories and sales plays. We called this sales enablement.

Working at Salesforce from 2005 to 2013 taught me a lot about hypergrowth and sales enablement. During those years, we trained, onboarded, coached, and certified more than ten thousand sales and customer-facing employees. We ran two boot camp classes a month. We certified our sales teams twice a year. We ran many sales kickoff events. We helped our sales teams be successful from the moment they were hired through celebration of their successes.

Our team tagline was "Hire to Hawaii." We embraced this tagline because we wanted everyone to know that we were in the business of helping our salespeople be the best they could be from the moment they were hired until the moment they sat on the beach celebrating their successes. Hawaii represented a sales reward for top performers. You were the best when you were recognized by your manager and peers and sent on a sales incentive trip. We knew what it took to deliver sales enablement excellence at scale. We were the founders of the enablement movement, and many of our present-day enablement leaders came from the teams that made it happen in the early Salesforce days.

The revenue results speak volumes to the impact that our sales enablement initiatives had on the business. Messaging alignment as a driver of revenue growth was the brainchild of Marc Benioff, and it worked wonders to extend a consistent brand experience from company vision to the website all the way to every customer conversation. The feedback from our teams over the years was always overwhelmingly positive. Teams appreciated the win stories, winning sales tools, and ongoing coaching. I knew there was tremendous value in curating content and coaching, and inspecting competencies with certifications and pitch assessments that we provided.

A Stroke of Insight

I spent time thinking that there had to be a better, more efficient way to get teams to be productive. It turns out every company and CEO want to get their teams more productive faster. After I left Salesforce, I put my thoughts into action on a journey to build high-performing sales teams at scale by improving knowledge, tracking effectiveness, and accelerating productivity. Then, we built a technology platform modeled around the proven sales enablement best practices that successfully took Salesforce from $300M to $3B in revenue.

Arthur Do and I cofounded SalesHood to help other companies with sales enablement. Our hypothesis was that the way to make training, onboarding, and knowledge sharing more effective and efficient was to provide bite-sized, mobile-enabled video content for teams and managers to engage in just-in-time social learning. The lessons we learned from our work between the years 2013 and 2017 are the foundation of this book.

The Naysayers Were Wrong

When we started talking about the value of salespeople sharing their pitches and secrets, most people reacted negatively.
They questioned why salespeople would be motivated to
share. "Aren't salespeople competitive?" they'd say. "What's in
it for them?"

We faced so many naysayers. Seasoned old-timer sales
executives wanted to jump on calls with their teams on a
regular basis or fly their teams to a central location to share
stories in person. Most venture capitalists were also nonbe-
lievers. I would meet with them to share the principles of
SalesHood and talk about the future of knowledge sharing.
Most would ask, "Why would salespeople do this?" Humbly,
I knew we were on to something when folks with limited
practitioner experience questioned our assumptions. I lived
the process of knowledge sharing for years at Salesforce and
saw firsthand how much of an impact it had on the success of
the company. I knew that sales professionals wanted to hear
each other's stories and winning plays.

Over time, the conversation shifted from negative sentiment to positive. More and more managers started believing.
Revenue results and data proved that we were right. More
leaders started executing and creating a learning culture.
Leaders began to see the benefits of more collaboration. One
particular moment that I remember changed everything for
me. At SalesHood in 2015, we ran a survey with a group of
salespeople, asking them what they thought of peer-to-peer
learning using video.[1] Here are the words they used:

---

1   The survey was conducted by Amy Pence at Alteryx in 2015. These words are a
     summary of the results.

Enlightening. Informative. Educational. Valuable. Impactful.
Collaborative. Innovative. Creative. Exciting. Educational.
Thought-Provoking. Insightful. Fun. Interesting. Motivating.
Amazing. Informative. Game-Changer. Fan-Freakin-Tastic [my
personal favorite]! Challenging. Galvanizing. Clarifying.

We learned that salespeople wanted access to each other's stories and knowledge. We realized the power of enablement to grow revenue. It wasn't only a Salesforce phenomenon. Our new challenge at SalesHood was to help other companies and teams align, coach, and collaborate more efficiently to grow their businesses faster, just as we did in the early days at Salesforce.

The process starts by defining enablement.

What Is Enablement?

Not too long ago, I received a text from a chief marketing officer at a company asking me for help: "Can you talk today? I want to ask you some questions about enablement best practices, roles, and responsibilities." I responded: "Let's jump on a call." A few minutes later we were exploring what was on his mind.

The CMO said: "I can't tell you how many times our employees aren't clearly telling the company story when they talk to our customers and prospects. Or they don't know where to find the tools and content they need to be successful." He added that his team spent hours and hours putting together the training materials and playbook to assist their sales and service teams.

Lack of enablement processes and lack of understanding

of the materials and training created by the product marketing teams are common concerns raised by executives, especially CMOs. Training and product knowledge content is created. Training workshops are hosted and attended. Emails share the myriad locations where recipients can find videos and tools to get up to speed. Yet sellers are still not on message, and they do not know where to go to get the tools and information they need to be successful. How can this be?

The conversation with the CMO quickly expanded to include sales leadership and the executive team. He described how the sales leadership team got pulled into the conversation and recognized the gaps. Everyone was on board to make the necessary changes. The enablement scorecard was high in certain areas and low in others. The areas needing improvement included planning, communications, and alignment with content publishers and subject-matter experts. The sales leadership team quickly responded to the CMO's statements with the words: "We do a poor job coordinating. All strategic initiatives need a strategic plan and strategic alignment at the highest levels." The teams aligned around the need to work better together.

The solution was not more or better technology, at least not for this problem. The challenge was that organizational expectations and alignment were not seamless between teams. This was a cross-organizational issue. It was also a communication issue and a planning issue. The teams were not planning together and agreeing on expectations and metrics. The teams were not making effective hand-offs. In fact, there were no documented hand-offs. A proven enablement framework helped.

Enablement is the alignment of people, processes, and

priorities with relevant learning, coaching, and communications delivered at the right time. Enablement is an organizational mindset and commitment to readiness and excellence starting with the CEO and touching every employee in your company. It is bigger than simply content and training. A well-thought-out and planned enablement strategy will bring departments and leaders together around shared priorities, metrics, and expectations. A well-documented and socialized plan will connect organizational dots and enable teams to work better and know who is doing what. Enablement is an all-company initiative involving sales, marketing, business development, partners, engineering, support, human resources, and leadership. Enablement translates messages and training delivered by subject-matter experts, at scale, for customer-facing employees, empowering them to have richer conversations with curious customers. Enablement is an organizational mindset and commitment to readiness and excellence. As enablement professionals, we empower our people to be the best they can be and improve their results with coaching, knowledge sharing, and mentorship that is scalable and measurable.

When done right, enablement is a big job. Often enablement leaders are quoted saying, "My job covers many departments." For some enablement professionals, their job becomes a place where companies incubate new ideas and undesirable initiatives. Enablement sometimes is the place projects go that no one wants to own. Enablement professionals quickly become administrators, logistical experts, and event planners. Enablement professionals are the ones working late and long hours to workshop agendas, playbooks, and training guides printed. We do it because we care.

Enablement is about helping teams onboard faster. Enablement is about improving effectiveness and productivity and measuring it. Enablement is about fostering a culture of learning where teams practice their skills. Enablement is about mentorship and creating a space for people to learn from each other. That said, not all enablement is equal. It is possible to do bad enablement.

What Is Bad Enablement?

Enabling your teams with training and content and working 24/7 doesn't mean the training, content, and long hours add up to the desired outcome. It's possible to do bad sales enablement. We see it all the time. Bad sales enablement looks and feels like a misaligned company with silos of education and knowledge sharing. You know it's bad when the sales enablement programs that are being created and executed are not aligned with senior leadership's top initiatives and priorities. You know your sales enablement is not great when it looks like the Wild West, with teams focusing on doing their own thing and deciding how they want to do it. Bad sales enablement is highly inefficient and ineffective. It's a recipe for friction and usually a sign of a bad culture. Having clarity go-to-market is a good way to align people, processes, and priorities and turn the tide from bad culture to great outcomes.

All too often, enablement professionals are doing enablement without truly understanding their company's go-to-market strategy. Their enablement programs aren't mapped to key performance indicators and metrics. You know your enablement is not working if sales processes are dated and not updated with the latest thinking from sales operations. When your certification is seen as a check box instead of true skills development and contributing to revenue, then you should know that your enablement program is not going to have the desired impact on your teams.

Look for the Signs

Bad sales enablement happens when sales teams and sales managers don't speak highly of their enablement people and the support they receive. You might hear phrases like "We're not getting what we need" and "Our enablement teams don't understand us." You can usually tell how your sales enablement program is doing and how they're perceived when you randomly ask one of your sales managers or salespeople what they think of their sales enablement team. Their face will light up with joy and gratitude if you're in a good spot. They'll wince or shy away from answering if things are not going well. Net promoter score is another indicator to see gage the sentiment and impact of your enablement program.

Self-Assessment

Here are some questions that will help you self-assess whether you're doing good enablement or bad enablement:

- How are your teams performing against their goals and metrics?
- What are you learning by correlating enablement and coaching activity to attainment data?
- How aligned are you with senior leaders on go-to-market priorities?
- When was the last time you talked with your front-line managers and their teams?

- How often are your stakeholders reviewing and approving your enablement calendar?

- How often do you meet the CMO to understand their marketing priorities?

- How is your relationship with sales operations, and when's the last time you updated your sales processes?

- How much of your boot camp and training content has moved to on-demand?

- What are your teams saying about the quality of your content?

- What do people say about you and your program when you're not in the room?

Keep the conversation and feedback loop open with your teams, and be ready to adapt your program if you're not getting the sense that you're having the right impact. Numbers don't lie. Don't be defensive. The great part of finding out that your programs aren't delivering value is that you can change very quickly.

First Ninety Days in a Sales Enablement Role

If you're new to the role of sales enablement or in your first ninety days in a new sales enablement role, here's a list of fifteen activities I would do if I were you:

1. Talk to as many salespeople and sales managers as you can to understand what's really going on in their territories and deals.

2. Sit in on real sales calls with customers and prospects to hear what buyers are saying. It's great to hear how the current pitch is received and how salespeople handle objections.

3. Interview top performers to find out why and how they're winning. Have them walk you through their winning deals. Review their emails and other sales artifacts. These are gold.

4. Do deal-win reviews to find out why and how you're winning new customers. Also do competitive loss-reviews to understand why you're losing. We all learn much from both our deal wins and losses.

5. Meet with leadership to understand their priorities and goals. Staying aligned with top executives is the way to stay relevant and current. Have the mindset to solve problems that are at the top of the list of your company's priorities.

6. Roll out a short video pitch challenge or customer storytelling contest to explore team engagement, confidence, and competence. Doing this will also create a crowdsourced library of best practices. It's a win-win and a quick organizational win for enablement professionals, too. Most company cultures don't do social learning well, so starting small is a great way to get started.

7. Meet with subject-matter experts like product managers, product marketing, competitive experts, marketing, and customer support to understand content strategies, product usage, and product release calendars.

8. Set up a monthly all-hands call cohosted by you and your sales leader to set a new tone and cadence of communications.

9. Partner with sales operations to map out your sales process, sales metrics, and Key Performance Indicators (KPIs). If the sales process is already written down, even better. Check with salespeople and sales managers to ensure it's current and relevant.

10. Crowdsource a list of sales conversations, pitches, and objections to overcome that move the needle in a sales process. These become future training and certification assets.

11. Sit in and observe how managers coach their teams in one-on-one coaching sessions. Also try and observe how managers run their weekly team meetings. Manager enablement is key, and it's all too often not part of an overall enablement strategy.

12. Evaluate the current sales stack to ensure the technology matches the go-to-market strategy. That said, don't spend your first ninety days working on RFPs (requests for proposals) and system evaluations.

13. Build a prioritized content, training, and onboarding plan by role. In the first ninety days, it's not expected that these plans are final. It's better to create draft versions that are socialized with leaders and stakeholders.

14. Document all that you heard and learned and present your findings, including the draft plan, to your leadership team for review, feedback, and buy-in.

15. Build a vision statement outlining your team's charter. Create a plan with metrics that is aligned with your company's top priorities. Make your vision broadly known across your company.

With so many competing priorities and initiatives, enablement leaders in a new job can quickly enter into a phase of being overwhelmed, ineffective, and complacent. I hope this list gives you focus and direction to be a transformational enablement leader.

I have a secret to share. After writing this down and collecting a lot of feedback from some very experienced enablement professionals, some of the most experienced ones I know haven't done what I'm recommending folks do in their first ninety days on the job. It's impossible to do perfect enablement all the time. Be mindful of what bad enablement is, and do the best you can to leverage these best practices.

KEY TAKEAWAYS

As you start building your team and working with other departments, have open dialogue about what enablement means to you. Create a conversation where people can discuss their experiences with enablement. Understand their mindset. Talk about what good enablement looks like, and talk about what bad enablement looks like too.

It's worth investing the time to use the self-assessment and questions discussed in this chapter to create a survey. It's always better to know where you stand and what your people think about your enablement processes and programs. If they think your enablement program is bad, then use the feedback and energy to make the necessary changes. Organizational sentiment of the enablement impact can be fickle, so always stay close to the pulse.

Chapter 2

Who Are Enablement Professionals?

The word "enablers" ignites images of connectors, knowledge makers, hard workers, doers, visionaries, evangelists, energizers, enthusiasts, educators, mentors, and believers. Enablers work hard and are also in thankless jobs. Enablers do whatever it takes to help others be successful. They make a difference.

Sales enablement professionals are a group of unsung heroes in corporations. They make the day-to-day work that helps go-to-market goals happen. They are known and depended on by all groups in a company—from sales, marketing, and product development to customer support and top executives. They strategize. They coach. They motivate. They train. They build tools. They help grow the business. They launch products faster. They are the go-to people in every team and department. The enablers are everywhere. They understand the processes that aren't documented. They know who all the players are. They are the last mile in product rollouts, campaigns, and initiatives. They know how to make things happen. They always get it done.

Some people may even affectionately call enablers "crazy." Steve Jobs said it best in his "Here's to the crazy ones" Think Different campaign. Inspired by the message, we created a similar mantra and video for the enablement profession for our 2018 MULTIPLIERS conference.[2]

Here's to the crazy ones. The doers, the coaches. The enablers, the culture builders. The revenue drivers. The ones who see things differently. They're not fond of losing deals. And they have no respect for excuses. You can believe them, disagree with them, celebrate, or curse them. About the only thing you can't do is be successful without them. Because they change things. They push teams forward. While some may see them as the crazy ones, we see enablement multipliers. Because the people who are crazy enough to think they can change the world are the ones who do.[3]

In this chapter, you will learn how to profile, empower, and recognize the early leaders who will drive organizational change. Who are these people? What makes them unique? How do you find them? How do you recruit them? How do you develop them? How do you mentor them? How do you inspire them to mentor each other? How do you find the future leaders you want to enable to become enablement masters?

---

2   SalesHood, "We are Enablement MULTIPLIERS," Youtube, Mar. 9, 2018, https://www.youtube.com/watch?v=Be-oOkJqqzQ.

3   Rob Siltanen, "The Real Story Behind Apple's 'Think Different' Campaign," Forbes.com, Dec. 14, 2011, https://www.forbes.com/sites/onmarketing/2011/12/14/the-real-story-behind-apples-think-different-campaign/6/#458ed0617f02.

"Q" the Enabler

The enablers who stand out to me are the doers of companies. They are the coaches, communicators, mentors, and connectors. They do good work because it inspires them. They are motivated to help their stakeholders be the best they can be.

Quyen Chang is one of these doers. She is an enablement leader with a proven track record in helping the fastest-growing companies get their employees ready and up to speed. When I spoke with Quyen, she shared that people call her Q because that was the name of the enabler in the James Bond movies. She said: "I am the enabler of employees in an organization." Q is a long-time enablement executive; some would call her a veteran. She worked at a time when enablement as a discipline was born and matured from training to a strategic view into the people, processes, and priorities that are created to support the professional development of teams with a focus on go-to-market.

Q has an interesting, diverse professional background. She is a business graduate from Santa Clara University. She spent time working as a retail associate while she was in school. A few years later she completed her MBA. She was hired on my team at Salesforce and started focusing her time enabling technical teams. She developed the framework and content for training and onboarding and helped make hundreds of technical professionals successful. She coached and guided new hires through their onboarding experiences. Her career continues to skyrocket. She leads global field readiness at one of the fastest-growing technology startups in the world.

Her background is similar to that of other enablers I know: results-oriented high achievers. They have real experience working with customers, communities, and constituents.

They are practical. They are hardworking. They always have an appetite to make things better. They have a diverse set of jobs in their career that can be tied together with an enablement theme. They are great storytellers. They are mentors. They are technical. They are not afraid to roll up their sleeves and do hard work. They work many thankless hours. Q is all of the above and an inspiration to us all.

How do we find and develop more people like Q in corporations? How do we make sure that every team, every department, and every company has their quota of enablers met? If we agree that having more enablers in our businesses will yield great results and build culture, then the next step is to recruit, develop, and mentor more enabler leaders.

Sheevaun and Her Four Pillars

Another great leader in the field of enablement is Sheevaun Thatcher. We worked together on many initiatives while she led enablement at Host Analytics and RingCentral. I asked Sheevaun her perspective about building successful enablement programs. Her philosophy comes down to four key pillars:

Strategic Alignment

Does everyone in the company know the strategy? How widespread is the understanding of the "why"? Understanding the "why" is what drives behavior and what creates culture.

Assets

What we do with these assets is create playbooks that are accessible in small, bite-sized chunks. Those assets will typically be sales collateral, videos, websites, podcasts, training modules, or whatever is needed to support the visual delivery of the "why". How current are these materials? Are they on message? How accessible are they?

Just-in-Time Content

We need to organize content so teams are provided with the right content when they need it, in the right format, at the right stage of the sales cycle in order to be successful. You have to think like a salesperson and create a system for "withdrawals" instead of the typical "deposit" document-management environment where files sit across many systems, collecting digital dust. It has to be quick and easy to access.

Tribal Knowledge

The best way to reinforce knowledge is by better team collaboration and sharing best practices, deal wins, and customer stories. It's important to create an environment that makes it easy for everyone to provide feedback and hear what's working and what's not.

Different Paths to a Career in Enablement

Enablement professionals have diverse backgrounds and come from all walks of professional life. I have met, worked with, and hired so many that I have a good sense of the most common career paths.

There is the salesperson who wants to accelerate their career to sales management, and they want to learn more about sales enablement and how corporations work. These salespeople usually have a track record of success, and they are ready to pause the grind of selling and hitting quota. The salesperson has a good perspective on what a salesperson needs. I remember sitting with one in an interview, and his answers to questions and comments about strategies were spot-on and added a fresh perspective to what we were doing. It helps to have firsthand experience in the role you are enabling.

The sales manager path is another common enablement professional track. Many sales managers like the opportunity to flex their coaching expertise and enablement knowledge. It's a good path for an aspiring vice president of sales. It is also good for a sales manager to get access to key executives and international expertise. I once had a sales manager reach out to me, and he ended up leading enablement for a new geography. It was a win-win.

Another enablement path is technical professionals who work with quota-carrying sellers. In B2B (business to business) enterprise sales, these are the people who do demonstrations and build solutions. They are good coaches and teachers. They know products. They are technically minded, and they are able to break down hard concepts into clear explanations. Many technical sales engineers become enablement professionals. They are systematic in their thinking, and that is good for programmatic enablement initiatives.

The learning and development group is another place where enablement professionals are born. They understand training and assessments. They build curriculum. While they may lack sales experience and context, they are good at driving learning outcomes and changing behaviors.

Enablement Professional Competencies

As I think about what it takes to be a successful enablement professional, I reflect on a wide range of experiences over my entire career. I think about what it took to achieve what we did at Salesforce and beyond at many next-generation hypergrowth companies. While it is hard to prioritize the competencies—as they are all important—it is worthwhile to try.

Great Communication Skills

Communications includes email, live, executive, and cross-departmental. Communications means being able to write headlines and copy like a journalist and being a great blog writer. It is an art.

You have to sell your ideas and enablement programs to your internal audiences. The key here is to write in a benefits tone and focus on the carrot instead of the stick. It is not easy. Pay close attention to this skill and develop it by taking a course or training. At a minimum, find a mentor who is strong in writing, and ask them to review your work and give you feedback. Also, asking marketing and copywriters for help is a great way to expand your skills and stretch new writing muscles.

It takes time, practice, and a lot of discipline to be great at communications, specifically writing. I once asked Chris Do, an Emmy award–winning brand and video storyteller, to speak at one of our customer conferences to elevate our enablement leaders' communication effectiveness. Chris talked about the importance of knowing your audience, keeping messages simple, and using images to accentuate key points.

Training Facilitation Mastery

Many of the best enablement professionals are energizing and motivational facilitators. It is hard to get in front of a room and command attention while at the same time educating and inspiring, but these skills are crucial. Content needs to have an impact. Stories need to be told. A good facilitator needs to be credible and authentic. When I facilitate a meeting or a conversation in a room, I am mindful of the need to be inclusive. It is important to keep everyone in the room engaged.

I have a general rule of thumb. There needs to be something to do or some kind of change of energy in the room every thirty minutes. The way to change energy is to ask a question or play a video or get everyone to do an exercise. Death by PowerPoint is not the path to great facilitation.

Culture-Building Abilities

Enablement professionals are at the heart and soul of the values of an organization. You create and nurture culture through storytelling and knowledge sharing. You take the best of the best and celebrate their behaviors broadly. That is how you shape culture. Whether you do it in video or written form, the art of sharing successes is a skill that must be mastered.

Excellent Storytelling Abilities

Personal stories are a great way for enablement professionals to connect. Storytelling is the way to accelerate learning by tapping into the emotional side of human connection. Everyone likes to hear and learn from a great story! The way to weave storytelling into an enablement profession is to use it as much as possible in all communications—over email, in person, on the phone, and over video conference.

Being a great storyteller takes discipline and practice. It is not hard to interview for the skill and also coach executives to do more of it in their day-to-day enablement work.

The book *TED Talks: The Official TED Guide to Public Speaking* shares the secret sauce of giving a great TED talk: storytelling. This book describes how executives use compelling customer stories to build trust. The starting point is having a relevant story that maps to what is top of mind to an executive or audience. Then match the story to the problem the executive wants to solve. As enablers, we need to link the problem to the story we are telling. Like in a TED talk, answer the question: What is the big idea you want to solve? Stay laser focused on that idea. Once you're anchored around one idea and problem, have the audience visualize how the problem can be solved.

When telling a story, lead with one big idea, and tell the story around that topic. Then take your audience on a journey by explaining the context. Share the steps to success with color and examples. Do a deep dive into the benefits of the idea, and engage people with an open-ended, engaging question.

Great Content Creation Skills

An enablement master needs to have proven ability to take ideas from subject-matter experts and create presentations, talks, knowledge-check tests, and learning paths. Successful enablement leaders are partially product marketers, and the good ones get it and do it well. Masters of content creation take ideas and present them in slides in a structure that is easily understood and consumed.

Cross-Departmental Collaboration Skills

Enablement leaders should be able to collaborate and work well with every department. They are the quintessential cross-departmental executive and connector. They can see the lines that should exist between departments, and they connect them. They connect sales with product teams. They connect support teams with product teams. They connect executives with employees.

Strategic Planner

Understanding the most important sales enablement metrics and being able to analyze what they mean is an important part of what makes great enablement leaders great. Being able to take the data and systematically drive outcomes to solve revenue problems is an important competency. Metrics help enablement leaders tie strategy to tactics.

Gravitas

The most successful enablement professions have gravitas and executive presence. When they walk into a room of learners or peers or senior executives, folks want to listen to them. They command respect. They are polished in how they present their ideas by knowing how and what to communicate to their audience. They are confident speakers and articulate.

Listening Skills

It's very important to be able to listen to your stakeholders. You want to be a great listener because you want to solve problems. You don't have to have all the answers. Take the advice of author, speaker, and marketing consultant Simon Sinek, who preaches the merits of being the last to speak.[4]

---

4   http://www.lasttospeak.com.

"You need to learn to be the last to speak," he says. You need to hear all views and empower people by giving them a voice. Being a great listener ensures you're solving the right problems for the right people at the right time.

Confidence

You know you are in a good spot and a trusted advisor when you can walk into senior leaders' office or send a text and share openly what's going on in the business. As enablement professionals, we hear and see all. It's our job to report back to our leaders the observations and sentiment from the troops. In some cases, we need to keep anonymity, and that's OK. Our job is to make sure our leaders are as much at the pulse of what's going on as possible.

Enablement Competency Levels

It takes time and experience to be an exceptional enablement professional. There are three levels to enablement professional excellence. The levels are additive.

1. The **foundational** competencies include: Communicator, Content Creator, Facilitator, Team Player, Confident, Authentic, Doer and Trust.

2. The **advanced** competencies include: Writing, Curriculum Creator, Storyteller, Coach, Listener, Achiever, and Motivator.

3. The **strategic** competencies include: Public Speaker, Program Strategy, Executive Gravitas, Strategic Planner, Culture Builder, and Visionary.

You can use these levels for hiring and career development of your team. Many of the enablement professionals whose stories we share in this book are strategic including foundational, advanced, and strategic.

Hiring Enablement Professionals

When looking to hire enablers, start by going back far into their careers to look for patterns of helping others. Have them describe some of their first jobs. How much did they over-achieve in school and in extracurricular activities? Individuals who had jobs when they were young tend to be conditioned to be enablers.

Here are some questions to ask a candidate or team member when exploring if they have the enabler DNA:

- What experiences do you have working with people?
- What did you study in university and why?
- What's the story of your professional life?
- Who are some of your early life influences and why?
- What were your first and second jobs?
- How did you rank in class?
- What were some committees and extracurricular activities you were a part of during school?
- What was your motivation to work part time during school?
- Who are your mentors? Who do you mentor?
- What are examples where you helped your team be successful?
- What motivates you to help others be the best they can be?

- What was your decision process to change jobs during your career?
- What are your experiences building content? What are some examples of content you created?
- How would you rate your training skills?
- What are some examples of training you have led?

The answers to these questions will start to paint a clear picture of the depth of enablement experience and mindset of professionals. You can learn a lot from what a candidate studied in school. A film major tells you they will be a great facilitator and storyteller. Engineers will be process centric. Look for specific mentorship and coaching experiences in their career. The value to you and your organization of finding out the answers to these questions is that you will find out the type of enablement person you will get. It will help you hire around them. You will find out if the enablement person you are talking to is going to be great at creating content or program managing a content-creation process. There is a big difference.

You should invest the time to figure out which kind of enablement professionals you need. Here are some profiles:

- Content creator
- Trainer
- Program manager
- Coach

You will try and find enablement people that have all the skills. I see it all the time in job descriptions. Be specific about what you need done, and have open, transparent conversations about what your candidate has done.

Building Your Enablement Brand

What matters most about our professional brand is what our stakeholders say about us when we're not in the room. Our competencies and our skills have a material impact on what people say about us. You should worry about your brand, because your brand will help you get sponsorship and resources for enablement initiatives you believe will move the needle at your companies. What does your brand do for you? What does your brand say about you and your team?

Linda Page, a senior enablement professional, shared her journey in a keynote at our conference in 2018. She talked about her career and how her brand helped her become successful. Linda kicked off her talk by asking a question: "How often as enablement professionals do we pause and think about, if there was an enablement hall of fame, what would our name plate say?" It was interesting to listen to Linda talk about what constitutes a good enablement and how to develop a brand. She used words like "authentic," "consistent," "trust," "simple," and "delivers" to explain potential brand qualities of enablement professionals.

Here's our collective challenge she posed during her talk: How do we as enablement professionals have a voice and say in decisions that are made by executives in the boardroom? How do we earn a seat at the executive table without a strong brand? For leaders, your personal brand will translate into your team's brand and the brand of enablement with other groups. It will set the tone for how you work with others, such as marketing and sales leaders. A great exercise to do on your own or with your team is to define your brand by defining your vision statement. Write your vision statement and then pin it up in your office.

Next, write a brand statement in one or two sentences. Have your brand statement answer these questions:

- Value: What are you the best at?
- Audience: Who do you serve?
- Unique Selling Point: How do you uniquely do it?

KEY TAKEAWAYS

Enablers turn ideas into action and results. They help enable teams to achieve results faster and with better cultural alignment. They have a good sense of how a company works. They are usually cross-departmental executives like salespeople, sales managers, product marketers, and/or trainers. These are the ones who have seen the big picture and understand the value in sharing cross-team knowledge and enabling others to strive for success. They know how to motivate people because they can speak the language of the different constituents.

Over the years, I have hired and recommended many enablers from different walks of life. They are consultative. They are empathetic. They are strategic. They are motivators. They solve problems. They get work done.

The key with making these hires is to know which one you are or you're hiring and then to augment them with coaching and resources. The ideal enabler is a blend of all the above who is empathetic to every role in an organization.

Enablers are the crazies, as explained by Steve Jobs. They have to be because they are solving top business problems for CEOs and companies. They are the heart and soul of many organizations. That is why we call them multipliers.

Chapter 3

Organizational Design

Leaders often ask me questions like "Where should enablement live inside an organizational structure and why?" and "How should we structure our enablement teams?" The answer to both these questions is "it depends." For many organizations, how enablement teams are structured and where they live are not standardized. These are a big unknown for many executives.

The factors that make it impossible to answer with certainty are the unknowns of the people, politics, and power base in the company. We need to look at the skills of our leaders and employees to understand where enablement can be most effective. We need to understand how decisions are made to ensure the organizational political realities will be an enabler of the enablement team's success versus a hindrance. And we need to understand where the power base is in the company. All these factors will guide us to create a better organizational structure. How we staff our enablement team and align our people with each other will be a big contributor to their success. The goal of this chapter is to explore the different organizational design scenarios and determine a way to decide what's best for you and your company.

Where Should Enablement Live?

There are many opinions about where enablement should live inside an organization, but there is no right answer. It can live in sales, marketing, or human resources. It can report to sales operations, or directly to the CEO, CMO, or CRO. I participated in an experiential workshop with other enablement professionals where we included enablement in product management to prove the point that enablement is a company-wide initiative. Some leaders of hypergrowth technology companies so strongly believe in the importance of enablement that they elevate the role to report to the CEO and call it the chief productivity officer. There is no confusion then of the importance of the enablement team in a company's go-to-market and culture.

If you put the enablement professional and team in the wrong department, goals will not be aligned and results will not be achieved. It's that simple. Organizational alignment (or misalignment) between sales and marketing and human resources depends on where enablement lives. It's also important to have clarity of scope so you and your teams will spend less time debating who does what and more time sharing progress on initiatives.

Where Did Enablement Live at Salesforce?

When I headed up enablement at Salesforce, I reported to Linda Crawford, who was the executive vice president of sales operations reporting to the chief sales officer, Frank van Veenendaal. For a short period at the beginning of my tenure in the role, I reported to the chief marketing officer, George Hu. When I stepped into the role as head of sales enablement, the role was in marketing, but it was quickly moved to sales. The reason for this change was based on the business priorities of the company. The year was 2007, and we were in hypergrowth mode. We were about to begin hiring more than twenty-five to fifty new salespeople every month. It made sense to align sales execution with enablement execution.

There was a bit of a mismatch when enablement lived in marketing, as our marketers had different priorities. I remember trying to meet the needs of sales while getting pulled in the marketing direction of demand generation and corporate marketing. The marketing staff meetings did not seem relevant to our goals of enabling our sales teams to be more productive faster. I talked to Frank van Veenendaal about the lack of focus on enablement and my growing list of marketing priorities. He asked Marc Benioff for the organizational change. There were no debates. It made total sense to everyone.

In this chapter, we'll explore where enablement fits and why and provide some scenarios to help decide what is best for your organization right now. We will also review how to map out an organizational structure for a global enablement team.

My experience at Salesforce and SalesHood and more recently working with more than one hundred companies and tens of thousands of sales professionals gives me great context to provide strategic recommendations for enablement organizational readiness and effectiveness.

Who Should Enablers Report To?

People always approach me with organizational structure questions: "Where should enablement live, and where do I want it to live?" The answers are not straightforward. In both scenarios, the answers are "it depends." It's important to begin the discussion with the scenarios and the pros and cons of each. The key here is to have a subjective conversation with a focus on the best interests of the company first.

Enablement Reporting to CRO/VP Sales

It is logical and expected to have the enablement team report to the vice president of sales. The most common and expected place to put enablement inside of an organizational structure is under sales. The benefits include alignment between sales priorities and enablement priorities, clarity of action, and shared accountability of metrics. When the enablement leader reports to the head of sales, the enablement team has direct access to sales leadership's ideas, thoughts, and priorities. The team can easily sit in on weekly team meetings and forecast calls.

Some of the negatives are accentuated when enablement supports many other employee roles. If a company is trying to drive an enablement strategy holistically across all roles, then you do not want to restrict scope. Non-sales groups will react negatively to being enabled by a sales enablement team. Roles such as services, customer success, and customer support or other roles inside an organization will say, "Hey, we're not a top priority for the enablement team. They don't get us." Impact and effectiveness will be lost. If the goal is to drive enablement across an entire organization, then I encourage you not to put enablement under the sales leader. Find another person to lead enablement, such as the chief marketing officer or the chief people officer.

When the enablement team is closely aligned with sales and does a great job, it's in the company's best interests to move them to another group to spread the knowledge and enablement best practices. It's recommended to build the center of sales excellence first, then scale it to other organizations. The sales credibility will be a huge driver of organizational buy-in and adoption.

PROS	CONS
• Aligns with sales leaders	• Excludes non-sales roles
• Leads by example	• May create the perception that it's only being done for sales
• Focuses on what matters	
• Facilitates getting resources and funding	

Enablement Reporting to Sales Operations

In some organizational structures, enablement lives in sales operations when that group is run by a strong leader. As companies mature and grow, it makes sense to put enablement under sales operations to inform priorities with data. My friend Jake Hofwegen, who is a very accomplished Silicon Valley executive, is also both an operational leader and an enablement leader. There are some significant benefits to having enablement map directly to sales operations. Getting close to metrics gives good focus and priority direction to the enablement team. Initiatives that are run and executed are measured against performance. I remember Jake telling me a story about being questioned by the leadership team on the impact of a sales enablement program. His answer was precise. The program he was executing had significant impact to the metrics defined by senior leaders and their shareholders. I like the alignment of metrics to enablement initiatives very much.

There is, however, a con to this organizational structure:

Under the wrong leadership and leadership style, enablement could be relegated to a training function and lose its impact and productivity punch. A vice president of sales operations with an enablement person under their organizational structure will potentially misrepresent and not highlight the real value of enablement. Investments will be at risk. We also tend to see sales operational leaders focus on metrics too much. (Yes, I said that out loud.) There is a human side to enablement that is a must, and sometimes the operational folks miss that part of the job.

PROS	CONS
• Uses a data-driven approach to enablement	• May be perceived as just training
• Is close to the metrics	• May create the perception that it's only being done for sales
• Uses one communication and calendar for enablement and operational issues	• Will not have a seat at the table
	• Will not have cultural changing, transformational impact

Enablement Reporting to Marketing

Even though in my early days at Salesforce we put enablement in the marketing organization, it did not make sense given the go-to-market and the personalities. That said, I really like the idea of enablement reporting to marketing. It's especially good when an organization has a complex product offering and product enablement is a key success driver. Organizations that have frequent product launches and releases, such as technology companies, will be served well by having enablement with a seat at the table. What I like about this option is the product marketers and subject-matter experts will be more mindful of the need to produce enablement documentation and coaching materials for their teams. When we think about the high value placed on fresh new content and how hard it is to get that content, we realize that we want more people who can create content to embrace enablement. By having the enablement leader sit on the staff of the chief marketing officer or a senior vice president of product marketing, better alignment will happen. A great enablement team and leader will bolster the perception and value of marketing to the organization.

The big con is better alignment will happen with marketing instead of the sales leaders. Another big con is that enablement will become out of touch with its teams by focusing more on content instead of coaching. With that said, in this group, the enablement team will be perceived as role agnostic.

PROS	CONS
• Aligns with content teams	• Gets deep into content and forgets skills and coaching
• Is role agnostic	
• Elevates the perception of marketing	• Results in less alignment with sales teams and revenue teams

Enablement Reporting to Human Resources

The idea of reinventing human resources is interesting to me. I believe our human resource people are in a wave of reimagining their roles and organizational manifestos. We are now seeing the chief people officer moving beyond compliance and harassment training and reviews to building culture and career advancements. Our human resources professionals are enablers. They want to be enablement multipliers.

If we look at a model company, Alteryx, a technology company headquartered in Irvine, California, revolutionizing business through data science and analytics, we see that sales enablement was at the center of their growth. They loved it so much that they promoted their director of sales enablement, Amy Pence, to director of enablement covering all roles and geographies. Amy's best practices are now being adopted by all the groups. She is now engaged at the CEO level and partnering with the head of human resources to execute enablement strategies focused on employee development and career planning. Employee engagement is now a key measure over and above productivity. As companies look to build a broader employee university or academy across all employees, partners, and customers, moving enablement under employee success and human resources makes a ton of sense.

PROS

- Emphasizes learning and assessments
- Helps scale by building templates and frameworks for all employee roles
- Creates culture
- Helps to reinvent human resources
- Makes CEO the top priority

CONS

- Creates a negative perception because of the bad rap human resources has
- Becomes simply a training team and loses impact of enablement
- Doesn't have the credibility to effect real change

Enablement Reporting to the CEO

Another scenario is up-leveling the function of enablement reporting to the CEO. There is no better seat at the table than the CEO's inner circles. I understand this is a more modern organizational structure. Dan Dal Degan (DDD), a close friend of mine, an advisor and former colleague from Salesforce, heard me speak about the merits of having the enablement leader report to the CEO. In my talk I called the enablement leader the chief productivity officer (CPO). As CEO of SpringCM (acquired by DocuSign in 2018), DDD then promoted his enablement leader, Gregg Reid, to chief productivity officer and ensured that the CPO had the CEO's endorsement and support for every initiative. At a macro level, having the enablement leader report to the CEO sets the right tone and expectation within the organization. It tells everyone this is an important and strategic initiative. The companies that realize revenue results faster are those that elevate the productivity conversation to the executive suite and engage their CEOs. The impact and value of the training, enablement, and communication programs built and executed by the CPO quickly expanded beyond sales and other customer-facing functions to the whole company.

The chief productivity officer gets along with all teams. Departments and executives feel listened to when they engage. Successful chief productivity officers are empathetic leaders. They understand or feel what another leader or team is experiencing from within the other's frame of reference. They see with the eyes of another, listen with the ears of another, and feel with the heart of another.

PROS

- Makes it a strategic imperative for the company
- Creates a greater likelihood that goals will be achieved

CONS

- Creates organizational friction with CMO and CRO
- Competes with chief of staff role

How to Structure Your Enablement Team

When you create the organizational structure for your enablement teams, you should consider how much enablement you will be delivering to your people and how much enablement they need. More complex products and more geo-distributed workforces will need more enablement. Here are some enablement-to-employee ratios to consider. For every hundred employees, you should have an enablement person. When products are more complex and new markets are being opened, you should overinvest in enablement and have ratios be as low as one for every fifty or even one for every twenty-five employees. When we opened the Munich sales office at Salesforce, we placed an enablement coach in the region, and they only had twenty-plus sales and customer-success professionals to enable.

In smaller companies—under a hundred employees—you can have one enablement person who wears multiple hats. The enablement person in a smaller company is accountable to deliver many of the learning and communications processes, such as training, onboarding, broadcasts, and playbooks. They should be able to do it all. Hire accordingly.

As the company grows, you'll start to organize around specializations by role and by process. For example, when companies grow beyond a hundred employees, up to one thousand employees, it is common to staff enablement professionals to build learning, communications, broadcasts, and playbooks by employee role. Specialization also happens with a person or two or small team focused on new-hire onboarding. We also begin to see enablement people focused on product training and competition. When companies grow, they enter into more dynamic markets, and employees require more product and competition coaching and enablement.

When we look at companies that look to scale beyond one thousand employees and up to five thousand, we'll see in-region coaches along with teams focused on customer engagement and sales process execution. At this stage of company growth, we'll see a mature enablement organization with a team divided by structure. We see an onboarding team, a coaching team, a product enablement team, a sales process team, and maybe a program management office focused on managing all the administration. Figure 3.1 illustrates what the team structure could look like at a larger company.

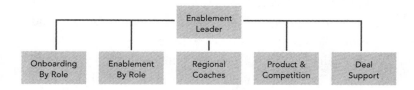

Figure 3.1: Large Company Enablement Team Structure

As a point of information, when I left Salesforce, we had about ten thousand employees. Here is what our enablement team looked like under my leadership. We had a team of eight to ten people focused only on new-hire onboarding. We had over twenty coaches in every major region, including the United States, Canada, United Kingdom, Ireland, France, Germany, Japan, Australia, India, and Singapore. We had a product enablement team of more than eight people that covered every major product. We had global sales and deal support teams focused on helping teams close more deals faster. The teams included common sales process aids like executive briefing centers, strategic account planning, industries, business case development, deal desks, and requests for proposals. Each pillar had a leader that reported directly to me. Because we lacked technology to scale, we also had a program office required to monitor and track all certifications and completion. I know we had a lot of people focused on enablement, and I founded SalesHood because I knew most companies could not afford to invest this much in building an enablement team and resources.

As you develop your own teams, keep your employee-to–enablement team member ratios in check, and use systems and technology to help scale your processes and priorities. Also, rely on your front-line managers to help you do more with less resources, especially in regions.

KEY TAKEAWAYS

Consider your goals, people, and executive personalities when evaluating where the enablement team should live organizationally and how to structure the team. The big conclusion is that the answer is "it depends." Enablement can live with sales or marketing. Put it in sales in the early days when productivity and metrics aren't being met. Move it to sales operations as the program and team mature. It can live in marketing if a company is quite focused on product enablement and releasing many products all the time. Keeping marketing accountable for enablement is a natural extension of the product marketing role. It's also OK to move it to human resources after a center of sales excellence is officiated and there is consensus around the organization that sales teams are leading the way to drive improved employee productivity. I'd be worried about moving a poor-performing enablement team to human resources, as they'll be relegated to curriculum design and learning and development. Whatever you decide, ensure all stakeholders understand their roles and execution expectations.

Enablement is a team activity. Done right, enablement brings teams together in a collaborative fashion to solve problems and improve employee productivity.

Chapter 4

Creating Organizational Buy-in

Being the catalyst of change for new ideas in an organization comes with great benefits and lots of hard work. New ideas can vary from a new sales process to a new sales training curriculum to investing in a new executive briefing center to hiring sales coaches to growing the enablement team to moving training center locations and more. These ideas are transformational and involve a lot of different stakeholder and organizational buy-in.

Uncovering problems to solve and championing is not for everyone. The political savviness required to make change happen is very high. We need to know how to communicate the vision of the idea without upsetting people who may already be quite married to the status quo. We need to co-build a business case with our executive sponsors to justify investment and action. We need to know how to engage with all stakeholders, especially the naysayers. The skeptics are the ones we have to win over before an idea gets squashed. The naysayers have to feel as though they have a say and are part of the team championing a new idea. Without them, ideas may never be executed.

In his book *Buy-In*, Harvard Business School professor John Kotter explains the importance of gaining others' support in order to create real institutional change:

> Buy-in is critical to making any large organizational change happen. Unless you win support for your ideas, from people at all levels of your organization, big ideas never seem to take hold or have the impact you want. Our research has shown that 70 percent of all organizational change efforts fail, and one reason for this is executives simply don't get enough buy-in, from enough people, for their initiatives and ideas.

In this chapter, we will explore the steps and tools to create and sustain organizational buy-in for enablement initiatives.

The Salesforce Training Center

The story I'm about to share is a great example of how enablement leaders can turn vision into reality. Many times during my career at Salesforce and afterward, people tried to convince me not to pursue an initiative. The words "it'll never happen" are said quite a bit at companies. It's too hard. It's too complex. It'll never get the support of leadership. It's too expensive. If you believe your idea is right and you have the business case to justify it, stick with your gut and make it happen. The rewards are huge both personally and professionally.

I was responsible for many strategic initiatives during my time at Salesforce. One of them, relocating the Salesforce Training Center, is a great example of the complexities around creating and sustaining organizational buy-in for a new enablement initiative. For years, the Salesforce "sales training boot camp" program was housed in a training facility off campus, in San Mateo. One of the main problems with it not being located in the Salesforce headquarters in San Francisco was that executives and product managers did not want to travel to it to motivate and inspire new employees.

We wanted our new employees to experience the culture in our San Francisco headquarters and walk away with a great sense of who we were. We wanted them to feel pumped up and jazzed about the company and culture. We spent hundreds of thousands of dollars every month flying them to San Francisco to then ship them to the off-campus location. It was a letdown. The survey feedback scored the content and agenda high but the location low. The quality of speakers declined month after month and ultimately lowered the quality of the program, which resulted in lower sales productivity. The business justification became clear. We needed to bubble up this initiative to secure funding from non-sales departments like finance, human resources, and real estate.

We started petitioning to move the new-hire boot camp program to San Francisco. The move impacted many organizations and budgets. Over an eighteen-month period, a cross-company committee that covered almost every department in the company met weekly. (Yes, you read it right; it took us over eighteen months to get to a positive decision.) The decision involved real estate, finance, human resources, sales, and marketing, and ultimately made its way to Marc Benioff's executive committee. It was that big and that political.

The steps to make the decision happen were extensive. We created a vision statement. We educated each stakeholder department on the value and business justification. We built a business case that included travel expenses and real estate costs. My team and I took charge of collating data and building spreadsheets. Our vision statement kept us focused on the "why." We created a business plan using the Salesforce "V2MOM" (vision, values, methods, obstacles, measures) framework. Every time we met a team and leaders, we shared the vision statement and the business case and showed an image of the new training center in San Francisco. One of the biggest benefits of this initiative was having everyone downtown, where we could connect people and culture. The quantifiable benefit was the faster ramp time we were expecting because of the increased participation of executives, product managers, and subject-matter experts.

Other initiatives that required the same level of buy-in included our sales process, building executive briefing centers, and growing a team of sales coaches. We followed a similar method to get organizational buy-in.

Anyone leading enablement will be faced with decisions. Where to focus? What initiatives need funding? How many initiatives can be done at once? What new projects will require more resourcing? What projects should stop because they have not had the expected impact? To get enablement initiatives funded and executed requires vision, business cases, advocacy, frequent communications, and the tenacity to stay the course.

Perseverance and tenacity are very important in driving organizational change. When you see something that can be improved, don't get overwhelmed. You can lead the charge to make it happen even if you don't have authority over all the resources and budgets. You have a clear picture of a better future. The question is, How do you get all stakeholders aligned? How do you integrate their ideas with your vision?

How do you make your vision their vision? Many great ideas fail because of poor communications and alignment of ideas.

Six Steps to Drive Organizational Change

Being a catalyst of change requires vision and persistence. John Kotter, in his book *Buy-In*, provides many thoughtful insights to help promote good ideas to happen. "Organizations don't prosper unless managers in the middle ranks identify and promote the need for change. People at that level gather valuable intelligence from direct contact with customers, suppliers, and colleagues."[5] There will always be resistance by people to support new ideas. Ideas happen by getting executives and middle managers to support them. Middle managers will always find excuses. Don't attack their opposing views. Be curious and understand their motivations. It's important to include these opposing views and people in the conversation and win them over.[6] Here is a six-step process to drive organizational change by aligning your people with proposed changes to your new processes and new programs.

Step 1: Draft a Vision Statement

The purpose of the vision statement is to begin to introduce a big idea to the executive level of your company to use to rally

---

5   Susan J. Ashford and James R. Detert, "Get the Boss to Buy In," *Harvard Business Review*, Jan. 2015, https://hbr.org/2015/01/get-the-boss-to-buy-in.

6   Good interview and discussion with John Kotter with many great tips to think about before your next big meeting, "Buy In: How to Save Good Ideas from Getting Shot Down," *Harvard Business Review*, Jul. 19, 2012, https://hbr.org/2012/07/buy-in-how-to-save-good-ideas.

everyone at all levels behind the idea. Putting a vision statement on a slide or in a document is an important step. It says that you are serious and that you have put some thought into the idea. It also shows that you are asking for collaboration and help.

Start by isolating the problem and drafting a clear, concise vision statement. Be clear on the problem and the benefits. The vision statement should be inspiring, inclusive, and action oriented. It should also outline metrics and a quantifiable benefit. Keep it in draft form to create a collaborative and inclusive process from the very beginning.

Anjai "AJ" Gandhi reached out to me in late 2016 to talk about a big initiative that he was leading at Ring-Central. He called me a few months after starting his new role as vice president of sales strategy and operations. The company was on a mission to extend its lead in the unified-communications-as-a-service market and break away from the competition. He said: "A key component was to develop a sales process methodology for optimizing our sales approach to the mid-market and enterprise segments."

We jointly crafted a new sales process methodology, refining it with sales leadership, and then developed a change management program to drive adoption. It was a big corporate ticket item and one that required significant funding and support from the senior executive team. This is the vision statement AJ shared with leadership: "Extend RingCentral's market leadership in cloud communications by improving sales productivity and accelerating growth."

AJ and his team worked with all segments of the business and key go-to-market partners (direct sales, channel sales, marketing, and customer success) to tailor the sales methodology to the needs of the business. The sales teams engaged in a one-week deep dive workshop to learn the new sales methodology and then conducted ongoing reinforcement huddles to practice and refine their skills. The program has made a big contribution to the accelerating growth and increasing sales productivity of RingCentral.

Another example of a great leader who tried to gather executive buy-in is Mark Siciliano. As vice president of sales productivity and effectiveness at Demandbase, Mark "sold his enablement vision to the highest levels in the organization." Mark asked for a meeting with the board of directors to share his vision of what sales enablement should be for Demandbase. This organizational alignment tactic resonated with the board and paved the way for great program success and faster business outcomes.

Step 2: Assemble a Diverse and Inclusive Team

Once you have some executive-level support for the draft vision, assemble a cross-departmental team representing a diverse set of opinions. The team should be inclusive but not exclusive. Set up an advisory committee. Kotter calls this step in the process "inviting in the lions." Look for a diverse set of opinions and people who will have objections. It's necessary to take a genuine interest in the opinions of stakeholders and not come to the discussion invested in a particular outcome. The committee should include a cross-section of roles and people and be set up to discuss and debate issues.

Step 3: Build the Business Case

The committee should build a well-balanced business case justification that includes a cost-benefit analysis. The committee should all be behind the business case. At a minimum, every enablement initiative should include the following committee members: sales managers, salespeople, and people from sales operations and marketing.

The business case should look at all quantifiable and non-quantifiable dimensions and prioritize the top metrics expected to make an impact. Look at metrics such as pipeline, win rates, average deal size, ramp time, and those discussed in chapter 6, "Go-to-Market," where I discuss metrics. Build a model that calculates the expected return on investment of your prioritized sales enablement initiative. What you are trying to do, why you are trying to do it, and what the expected return will be should be crystal clear.

Another way to look at the business case is from a sales headcount perspective. What will deliver more return on investment: another quota-carrying salesperson or using that money to drive an initiative? These are the kinds of open and transparent conversations you want to have when discussing the business case. Make the ROI clear, and communicate it to all stakeholders. There is no reason to be shy about the business impact you expect to see. That is the ultimate tool to gain organizational buy-in for your top sales initiatives.

Step 4: Communicate Frequently

Communication needs to be frequent and crystal clear. A constant drumbeat of communications is critical to keep momentum going. A regular weekly update summarizing progress and next steps is a smart tactic. Be consistent in communications. If the project is ongoing, send an update every week at the same time. If progress isn't being made, don't skip a communication update. Once a decision is made, it is time to get posters and banners and start promoting the merits of the initiatives. Communications is as important in the pre-planning, planning, launch, and ongoing. Don't let your ideas and initiatives go sideways with suboptimal communications.

Step 5: Be Hands-on with Stakeholders

An important step is to work with the stakeholders, hand in hand, to show them what their world is going to be like. For real estate facility improvement, like my Salesforce training center initiative, take people on tours. If you're rolling out a new sales process, sit on some calls with salespeople to show them how the process works. If you're working with marketing to publish a new product playbook template, do the first one with them until they are comfortable with the process changes.

My friend Bob Kruzner, the director of sales enablement at ServiceMax shared a great strategy he does with his sales teams to ensure buy-in. It is both tactical and powerful. Over the years, Bob has rolled out many new systems and programs and finds that buy-in breaks down when people are not trained and onboarded properly. He mentioned an experience where he was personally trying to use a new system, and after the roll-out he felt as though the company spent so much money to fund the project and failed at the end by training him on how to use the system. "We have this new tool," he said. "I don't know how to use this new tool. We made this big investment, and we never got trained." He took this lesson and now makes sure that he drives personalized and hands-on training for educational and buy-in purposes. In his sales enablement program at ServiceMax, he walks his salespeople and sales managers through new-hire onboarding. He goes step by step to explain the intent to his people. Once people get it, they buy in. "A light goes on, and then I know we have them," Bob said.

Step 6: Keep the Momentum Going

Finally, focus on sustaining organizational buy-in. Avoid the shiny new penny syndrome and stay the course. Do this by carrying the initiative across the finish line and then sticking with it. Revisit the vision and goals of the initiative that was approved and in action. Set a quarterly or monthly team review. It takes time for new initiatives to stick and become part of the fabric of a culture and company go-to-market. Enablement professionals are great at sticking around and making sure initiatives are working as planned. Conduct surveys post launch to make sure the intent and sentiment are aligned with the vision and goals.

Many organization-wide initiatives fail because they lack a champion owning the last mile. I was having lunch with Laurie Schrager, vice president of sales operations at Tealium, and she commented that enablement professionals are successful because they do "full-swing program execution," meaning they carry all initiatives across the finish line and ensure the work is done to plan.

Understanding Stakeholder Motivations

Enablement leaders need to understand and cater to many stakeholders in bids to drive transformational initiatives that require cross-departmental organizational buy-in. Each stakeholder has their own motivations, expectations, and communication styles. Tailor your approach and messages to each role and persona.

Executive Stakeholders

When you seek to secure organizational buy-in, you must win over top executives like the CEO, COO, and CFO. They want decisions to be made thoughtfully and quickly. They love when problems are presented to them with solutions that already have consensus. Your executives expect clear, concise, data-driven communications. When you present an idea or share a point of view with your top executives, do not start with the detail. Open up the communications with the headlines. Explain the "so what" first. Communicate to your executives as though they are skimming the headlines in a newspaper. Speak to the big-picture, macro level first. Have the detail ready if your top executives want to drill down to learn more. Also, when working with a CFO, it is important to have mastery on the numbers and financials. Know your audience.

Another stakeholder you will work with a lot is the vice president of sales. Arguably, they are the most important stakeholder, and you are employed to serve them. If your vice president of sales is not making money and is not performing at the expected level, they will not last long in their role. Being clear on that reality is important. They are motivated by quota and revenue goals. They expect everyone around them to help them sell more. A sales VP is interested in closing more business. Be mindful about what their challenges are. If they are behind in hiring, do not walk into their office to talk about initiatives that do not help recruit more salespeople. If they are short on pipeline, then follow the same rule and avoid talking about anything but ways to build pipeline.

If you have to get their mindshare, make sure they are in a good space. There is nothing worse than approaching a sales VP with a great idea at the wrong time and losing credibility and momentum. Timing is everything with sales VPs. When presenting ideas or initiatives, make sure to explain to the sales VP what it means to them, their goals, and their teams hitting more quota faster.

Working with marketing and CMOs is quite different than sales. Marketers have different priorities. They are focused on product launches, communications, advertising, public relations, marketing events, branding, and campaigns. CMOs and marketers want to be efficient about helping sales be successful. You need to be respectful that marketing has their next big thing right in front of them. Just like sales has a monthly, quarterly, and annual rhythm and business reality, marketing has their own. Know what is on their marketing calendar, and align with their schedule for review meetings and brainstorming. The message that is hopefully coming out loud and clear is that when you work with stakeholders, you should be mindful of their priorities and schedules.

Sales Managers

Engaging and getting buy-in from sales managers is critical too. You'll find that sales transformation initiatives lacking complete buy-in and support of the front-line managers will be challenged from day one. They are responsible for hiring, training, coaching, building pipeline, and closing business. They are overworked, and they are usually chasing their monthly and quarterly numbers. Setting up a meeting on the busiest day or during the busiest time of the year is not a winning strategy to secure buy-in from this group. The sales manager is a great person to engage early and often when you are drafting strategies for sales enablement programs. They are usually former top-performing sales executives. They are looking for new challenges, and front-line sales management is a logical path. You should always have a core group of sales managers on speed dial to keep you honest. They are a great set of folks to brainstorm ideas. Some of my most fond professional relationships from my time at Salesforce are with front-line managers. Until this day, we help each other.

Salespeople

Another group of stakeholders for you to consider when creating and sustaining organizational buy-in is salespeople. You should prioritize and create programs based on what salespeople need. A data-driven point of view is important. It also helps to always be at the pulse of what your salespeople need and what they are thinking. When your CEO calls you or your VP of sales calls you, rest assured they will ask, "What's going on in the ranks? What are our salespeople thinking?" It is always good to have a point of view and examples to back up what you are sharing. Trust me, the call will happen. You want to always be ready.

Regarding organizational buy-in, you should be clear on the value to the salesperson and be able to answer their question, "What's in it for me?" If you do not address their needs and communicate why they should care, you will never have a successful rollout of whatever you are trying to do. Set up committees that you can tap into when you have questions, and have a few salespeople on speed dial. As a salesperson, I care about closing more business with less work. Salespeople want shortcuts to success, and they want the secrets of success, now. Know this as you tailor your vision statement and business case and communicate value.

As a tip, do your thinking on each stakeholder's most common objections. Write them down. Role-play them with your team. Create a slide for each one. Be prepared to show the slide(s) when you are meeting your stakeholder. It is always better to lean into an objection to better understand the real motivation of the objection instead of getting defensive. You need to apply some sales fundamentals like objection handling to secure organizational buy-in. The trick is to uncover objections to avoid surprises.

Getting Ready for the Big-Decision Meeting

Here are some tips that will help you avoid any big organizational buy-in surprises. Let us assume you have a final decision meeting or final presentation meeting planned. You have spent weeks, months, maybe even years planning and preparing for the big meeting. Whether it is a meeting with the CEO, or top executives are coming together to vote on your initiative, it is important to be clear on what you want to achieve in the meeting and avoid small talk.

I also highly recommend that you know the outcome of the meeting before you walk into the room. It might seem devious, but it isn't. Know who will be in the room and do these actions with every person:

1. Schedule a meeting at a reasonable time for everyone.

2. Talk to your meeting participants one-on-one about the meeting goals.

3. Send them a brief explaining the meeting goals.

4. Ask them if they have any objections or concerns. Be curious.

5. If they do, answer them. The last thing you want is any major obstacles coming at the end.

6. Share the presentation with each person before the meeting.

7. Walk into the meeting knowing what each person is thinking.

8. Bring printouts of the necessary slides and materials as a courtesy for folks to flip through during the meeting. It's old school, but folks appreciate it.

9. Do not get defensive if things go wrong. Be professional.

10. Send executives a handwritten card after the meeting, thanking them for their support.

Treat the meeting and the decision just like you would handle a sales cycle. Follow all the best practices that a professional salesperson would if they were working on closing a big deal.

KEY TAKEAWAYS

I had a lot of fun writing this chapter. It forced me to think about all the sales enablement initiatives I worked on and to realize that one of the big reasons some did not do well is that I did not secure the right organizational buy-in. My big takeaway is you should not assume anything. Organizations and teams have so many competing priorities. Follow the six steps to secure and sustain organizational buy-in: draft a vision statement, create authentic and diverse advocacy, build the business case, communicate frequently, be hands-on with stakeholders, and keep the momentum going. Do not forget that driving big sales transformation involves people who want to be heard and feel as though they have a say in their future.

PART TWO

PROCESSES

Chapter 5

The Enablement Process Map

In the context of complex organizational structures with silos and people racing to get their work done, where is there a definitive Enablement Process Map? The challenge is there are so many moving parts to executive company enablement. There are so many points of failure. Here is a question I get over and over: Who does what and when?

Think about a regular product launch or a website branding initiative. Companies spend huge amounts of funds to develop new products or launch a new corporate website. Resources are allocated to do the work. Teams huddle up to execute the plans, and they deliver. In most companies, the idea of enablement is an afterthought. After the product launch or after the website launch, folks on the project look at each other and say, "Well, it probably would have been a good idea if we enabled our employees and sales teams on this." Everyone is well intentioned. It's not that enablement was maliciously excluded. It just never bubbled up as a top priority and conversation. That someone is taking care of it is a thought that sits in the back of everyone's mind.

Enablement is a company-wide initiative requiring a standard operating procedure supported by a clear outline of processes. We need an Enablement Process Map. Our teams and our leaders need to visualize what enablement looks like and how it works. It can't be something that we tuck away in the corner or do as an afterthought. It needs to be the center of our business strategies and tactics. I went on a multiyear journey to create the Enablement Process Map.

Inspired by Pragmatic Marketing

When I was early in my career, I was introduced to the Pragmatic Marketing Framework designed for technical product marketers. It worked well for me when I first moved to San Francisco and started working as a product manager in Silicon Valley. The framework showed me what I needed to do to be successful and also gave me the organizational context to understand how I impacted the business. I carried the Pragmatic Marketing aid with me to meetings. I pinned it up at my cube. I took it with me from job to job. I referenced it when it was time to build a new business plan or product plan. It was my Silicon Valley bible. My experience with the product marketing process map created by Pragmatic Marketing inspired me to create one for the enablement profession.

I wasn't alone. My fellow product managers and product marketers all loved it and used it too. What was great about it was that teams who used it and followed it were immediately on the same page. Everyone always knew what needed to get done. It provided a standard language for getting work done.

Overview of the Enablement Process Map

The enablement processes represent what we do to achieve our revenue and business goals. We need to use different processes to accomplish different business outcomes. The framework works left to right and top to bottom. We want to start by defining and codifying our processes and turning them into learning programs and content to be used in customer engagements. We want to close the loop by correlating attainment to activities and celebrating achievements. We want to focus on the most basic strategies and tactics first before we go into advanced and mature initiatives. That's how the left to right and the top to bottom is designed to work.

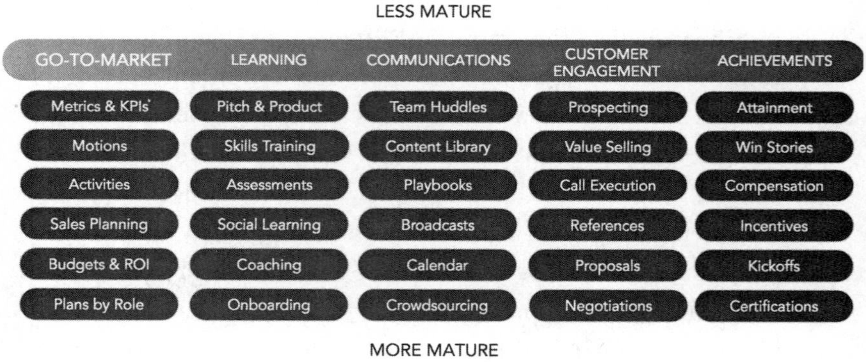

LESS MATURE

GO-TO-MARKET	LEARNING	COMMUNICATIONS	CUSTOMER ENGAGEMENT	ACHIEVEMENTS
Metrics & KPIs'	Pitch & Product	Team Huddles	Prospecting	Attainment
Motions	Skills Training	Content Library	Value Selling	Win Stories
Activities	Assessments	Playbooks	Call Execution	Compensation
Sales Planning	Social Learning	Broadcasts	References	Incentives
Budgets & ROI	Coaching	Calendar	Proposals	Kickoffs
Plans by Role	Onboarding	Crowdsourcing	Negotiations	Certifications

MORE MATURE

Figure 5.1: The Enablement Process Map

Go-to-Market

A well-thought-out and executed enablement strategy happens when we have everyone in our go-to-market teams aligned on the same messages, metrics, and motions. You need to know what your vertical strategy is, too. It all starts with intimate knowledge of why your customers are buying and why you're losing deals. Win and loss analysis serve as the foundation for all go-to-market enablement processes. The metrics and key performance indicators of the business follow. They must be documented and agreed to by all stakeholders and measured and shared frequently.

There is no way to deliver a scalable and repeatable enablement program without a well-documented sales process and sales methodology. It is important to codify motions, such as the sales process, territory planning, account planning, and quote to cash. It is critical these are available for teams to review, approve, learn, and execute. The processes need to leverage best practices and consider the uniqueness of company culture and go-to-market. The most fundamental motion is the sales methodology. You need to document it if it isn't already written down.

From the sales process will emerge activities that everyone will execute together.

Before embarking on a new enablement initiative, ask the question: What problem are we solving and why? Get clarity around key performance indicators (KPIs) like win rates, deal sizes, time to close, time to first deal, time to ramp, attainment, pipeline generations, and bookings, to name a few.

It is important to be clear on how much investment is being made and how much is needed to achieve the goals that are core to the business. When I was at Salesforce, we spent more than forty million dollars a year on enablement. We were investing heavily during the hypergrowth years. Understanding the spend and resource allocation will help prioritize what metrics and KPIs are prioritized. We cannot enable every one equally, so we must decide how best to allocate funds and budgets. An extension of the budgeting process is systems. What systems are needed to support the growth and goals?

The more mature organization will take all this information and begin creating plans by role, which looks at the needs and requirements of all employees and stakeholders. An advanced organization with complex geo-distribution and segmentation and many products will need to have plans by role or they will not achieve their go-to-market goals.

Learning

It's proven that people learn from the best. Create a culture of teams learning together and from each other. Share win stories and winning sales presentations regularly. Use technology to do this at scale with peer reviews, and use old-fashioned round-table conversations to facilitate the sharing of ideas.

Partner with subject-matter experts to build the right training and onboarding to educate, energize, and enable your employees. Improve the competency and confidence of your teams by creating learning paths by role. Map job expectations, learning curriculum, and career progression. The learning paths should be introduced in new-hire onboarding and refreshed as career milestones are hit or missed.

Active learning is a surefire way to get teams to internalize new content. Make learning relevant and impactful by applying learning to real-life scenarios and real deals. If you roll out a new product playbook, then why not have your teams practice and apply the new product positioning to existing deals? Why not do some persona prospecting and position the new offering to active prospecting accounts? That's how we apply learning by doing.

The first step in creating a scalable, revenue-generating sales onboarding plan is to align on metrics. We all want to front-end the process with metrics that help sales to focus on the right behaviors and actions. For example, we want to measure pipeline generated, time to first deal, and time to quota attainment. We should create new-hire onboarding programs that blend self-paced work with certifications, team-based exercises, and role plays. Focus all activity around what is most important to be productive and successful in an employee's first thirty days.

A big part of an employee's development is to have the right skills. As enablement leaders, our job is to help our teams be the best they can be by giving them the skills training they need to be successful. Every employee has their own set of skills needed to do their jobs and develop their careers. Create a skills map that is tied to job descriptions and career pathing. Salespeople need more foundational sales training from prospecting to asking open-ended questions to negotiations. Developers need more from coding to development languages to quality assurance. Each employee and role have their own skills needs.

Coaching should happen between managers and their teams and between peers all the time. Ongoing training is sometimes called coaching too. As enablement leaders, you want to help your managers do more and better coaching.

Communications

Keep content engaging, bite-sized, and rich with storytelling. It's important to have a clear inventory of the content that exists and needs to be created. The list includes personal playbooks, product briefs, corporate presentations, customer stories, and competitive battle cards. The corporate pitch and company overview presentation are important to document and make readily available to teams. There should be different versions depending on the role and how much customer-facing time the employee has in their day-to-day job. This content forms the foundation of training and onboarding.

Additionally, customer stories are great to bring the company pitch to life with a strong customer voice. Customers describe value better than we ever could. Injecting customer stories early and often into the enablement plan of employees sheds light on value and creates real emotional loyalty. It is helpful in explaining to your employees why they are working so hard and why they're doing what we're training them to do.

Customer Engagement

The customer engagement processes are important for teams to follow. They are a direct extension of the go-to-market processes. Our teams should be trained and coached on them. They should have full access to content and assets so they can spend more time selling and less time searching.

We help our teams self-source more pipeline with best practices on reaching out to the right prospects with the right messages at the right time. Our job is to make this process more efficient. We help our teams build relationships and uncover new business with storytelling, discovery, and flawless sales execution. We help our teams close deals faster with winning proposals and instruction on how to make their executive presentations more compelling. In more advanced organizations, we'll formalize the deal-review process and the account-planning processes to build more predictability and consistency across every step in our customer's buying journey. We want to enable our people to be more curious, better storytellers, and more empathic to ultimately elevate costumer engagement.

Achievements

The enablement processes that matter the most and are forgotten all too often relate to achievements. We tend to not celebrate the wins enough. We do not invest the time to correlate achievements to activity so we have a better sense of what is working and what is not.

Achievements are about aligning behaviors and activities with rewards and compensation. It's about taking your team out to dinner to celebrate a big win, and it's about showing gratitude with simple things like saying thank you. How achievements are communicated and celebrated say a lot about the culture of your company. As an enablement leader, it's your job to keep this top of mind and make sure the rewards and recognition are flowing at the right times and in the right quantity.

How and When to Use the Enablement Process Map

We created the Enablement Process Map to help drive more cross-team collaboration and conversation. It is a great resource to use in a kickoff project involving cross-company departments. Pull it up on a big screen, or share screens during a video conference and engage the team in a conversation. You can also print it out for everyone meeting in person. Talk about what each box means and who owns which box. Use it as a map to define role and responsibilities. Use it as a map to hold teams accountable for deliverables. Color code if certain teams like marketing or sales or products or human resources own different boxes. Use it to spread the work and ownership of enablement tasks so everyone has a part to play.

KEY TAKEAWAYS

The Enablement Process Map is a blueprint of the key activities needed to create a company-wide culture of enablement. Each pillar represents how we achieve our enablement goals.

The pillars include—

1. Align Go-to-Market

2. Nurture Learning

3. Share Compelling Communications

4. Elevate Customer Engagement

5. Celebrate and Correlate Achievements

Chapter 6

Go-to-Market

Enablement professionals are super talented and creative individuals. We always want to help everyone. It's in our nature. We don't know how to say no. Sometimes we create training, content, and enablement programs without truly understanding the "why." That's the purpose of this chapter. The Enablement Process Map sits on top of the assumption that we have a clear understanding of the go-to-market. We need to understand our company's metrics, revenue, and profitability. We are clear on geographic expansion and hiring goals, and we also know where to spend time. We focus on segments and teams that drive the most revenue, and we focus opportunistically on groups and geographies that represent growth potential.

I have put a lot of thought into why we as an industry aren't leaning into the analytics to create a data-driven enablement culture. After speaking with hundreds of sales enablement professionals, I've concluded that there are three reasons why we are uncomfortable with the enablement metrics causing misalignment with the company's go-to-market priorities:

- Not having access to the data
- Not knowing the metrics that matter
- Not knowing how to present the "so what" of the data

Every company looks at metrics a little differently. Some use Salesforce. Others use Excel. Others use analytics tools. Each leader has their own scorecard. Enablement professionals need to be part of the conversation about what is working and what is not. We need to connect the dots between the great work we do and the results. We want to be able to walk into our leadership's office and show the correlation between performance by seller and by team and enablement activity. We need to be able to turn a subjective dialogue into a fact-based and analytical conversation. We need to be able to provide answers to the most important question: What can we do to improve performance and achieve our go-to-market goals?

Missing the C-Suite with Metrics

I remember in the summer of 2012, six months before I left Salesforce, preparing for an executive-level review of Salesforce's sales enablement strategy. Invited to Hawaii to present to the president's committee and about a hundred senior leaders, my team and I created a presentation to showcase our priorities for the coming year. It missed the mark.

After my second slide, Marc said: "Show us a progress report by territory and role of our team's messaging certification accomplishments compared to attainment." I had a plan to get that, but I didn't have it ready. Marc was not happy.

"Why are we not systematically certifying our teams on the latest messaging?" he asked.

We were, but the answer did not matter. I did not come

prepared with the data showing it and showing the correlation. It did not matter that we had done it year over year and quarter over quarter. What mattered was that I was focused on a different agenda than Marc and not focused on data and attainment.

It did not take long for me to realize how awkward this meeting was going to be. I remember being so uncomfortable and hot that the sweat came through my Hawaiian shirt. I half-jokingly asked if I could go jump in the ocean and Marc said yes. I learned a lot from this experience.

Marc and I met later that day and worked on a plan for me to share the right information. He also shared his goal to reinforce the importance of measuring the right success metrics and ensuring that we had alignment across all teams.

Guidance on Enablement Metrics

We can spend a lot of money and use a lot of resources to run sales enablement initiatives and programs without knowing what is working and what is not. Since you are an enablement professional always willing to do what it takes, you often end up doing too much. Burnout is a real concern. But you can use data to set expectations and do the right work at the right time. Data does not lie.

Here is a typical conversation I have with enablement leaders that indicates why we need to elevate this discussion and revise our thinking.

Enablement Professional: We have an onboarding problem. How can you help us?

Me: Why do you think you have an onboarding problem?

Enablement Professional: We have to onboard ten new salespeople this year, and our track record is far less than stellar. We have not been able to get new hires ramped up and productive fast enough.

Me: How many total salespeople do you have?

Enablement Professional: We have over one thousand salespeople.

Me: What is their sales attainment year-to-date?

Enablement Professional: We are seeing about 40 percent of our sellers hitting quota. [For the record, most enablement professionals know they have a problem, but they are not prepared to discuss the details of the data because they are not part of the data conversations.]

Me: You do not have an onboarding problem; you have a sales attainment problem.

I have this conversation three to four times a day. We often are not focused on the right metrics, and we do not know where to look for answers. Data and initiatives that drive change remain siloed.

As sales enablement professionals, we need to have clarity about the problems we are solving. Access to performance data and transparency around attainment metrics help us to get aligned with senior leaders. Clarity stops us from doing busywork instead of the work that really matters. It helps us be better enablers. It helps us justify the work we and our team do.

Top Sales Enablement Metrics

We need to understand and use the following metrics to align our people, processes, and priorities and achieve our go-to-market goals.

QUOTA ATTAINMENT

Quota attainment is a measure of sales rep performance. The top deliverable of sales enablement is to help bring salespeople to peak performance. We measure whether our teams reach their sales targets in a given period. If they have reached their goal, they have attained quota, or if the team has only achieved 50 percent quota attainment, then half have reached their quotas. Any time our sales enablement program lifts our team's ability to hit quota, top-line will be massively impacted.

Know this number, and know where you stand as an organization.

The way this number is calculated is by looking at attainment by role. A quota-carrying sales professional should measure new revenue closed in a given period of time. Account managers should measure upsell revenue closed and renewal business. A sales development person should measure leads converted to new qualified opportunities or meetings scheduled with qualified buyers. The way to calculate these numbers is to look in your sales system of record.

The next step is to correlate attainment with activities. Look at the teams and people that have hit their quota or not hit their quota. Look at their respective coaching and consumption enablement activity. Look for patterns and trends. If your teams that hit their quota numbers also did the most coaching and consumed the most content, then you will prove your work is making an impact.

In your process, I recommend reviewing these numbers monthly, quarterly, and annually by seller, manager, segment, and tenure. Pay attention to the distribution of people who attain their quotas. The percentage of salespeople who hit quota is an important metric. It highlights a healthy business if the numbers of people hitting their quota sales attainment is greater than the people who are falling behind. What you want to avoid is a small number of people crushing their numbers and carrying the team. That is not a healthy state of a business.

WIN/LOSS RATIO

We want to help our teams always beat their external competitors. Know the win/loss ratios of the deals you pursue against those of your competitors by team, manager, and seller.

WIN/LOSS RATES

To calculate your winning percentage, add your wins and losses together to get the total number of deals closed. Then divide your number of wins by the total number of deals. Know deal-win rates to better predict resources, leads, and deals your sales team may need to hit quota.

SALES-CYCLE TIME

The number of days in a sales cycle helps a company accurately predict revenue and forecast. When deals take longer than expected, look for clues as to why. Perhaps the seller is not executing the sales process effectively or not following the sales playbook. It is good to look at sales-cycle time in aggregate and by sales stage conversion to uncover where salespeople are struggling in the sales process. It is your job as an enablement professional to recommend coaching and content to your salespeople. Knowing where in the sales process your teams are getting stuck or need help is a great way to prioritize where to start resourcing more enablement.

DEAL SIZE

When salespeople sell value by taking their customers through the sales process and the buyer's journey, they close bigger deals. Why? The questions and relationship building results in higher values and less discounting. Knowing the winning actions of the team members that accomplish these steps is another enablement metric to measure and influence. Look at deal size and average selling price to gauge the sales skills of selling value and negotiating. Great sales content and sales training are both key levers you want to influence with targeted coaching and content.

TIME TO RAMP

Cutting down the time to ramp, or how long it takes to train new hires to perform independently, is one of the primary parameters that can help to prove the effectiveness of onboarding efforts. This onboarding metric is a critical one to clearly measure and define. It is broadly measured by the amount of time it takes new hires to be fully productive. For salespeople, time to ramp means the amount of time it takes to hit quota. Other metrics measure leading indicators, such as off-ramp quota and time to first deal and time to second deal. I suggest looking for early indicators to avoid finding out too late that your teams are not being productive.

EMPLOYEE ATTRITION

Employee turnover is a big, costly problem in corporations today. Employee retention should be a top metric and priority. Organizations spend billions of dollars hiring, recruiting, and developing people. You need to know how many employees are leaving your company each year to understand the true cost of employee attrition. Do not forget to include the opportunity cost of deals not closed during that time period.

CONTENT EFFECTIVENESS

Knowing which content is working and which is not is important to sales and marketing leadership. Tying knowledge and content consumption back to closed or lost deals is the holy grail of content enablement metrics. Content consumption metrics, such as content views, file downloads, and user ratings, should be compared to revenue. This can help marketing and subject-matter experts know if their work is making an impact. The combination of content consumption data with revenue data and CRM data will begin to tell a story around what content may have led to a closed or lost deal.

EMPLOYEE ENGAGEMENT

More and more, companies are realizing that their employees are not engaged in their professional and career development and, worse, may feel as if their managers are not engaged either. There are a couple of ways to measure this kind of engagement. You can measure employee satisfaction or net promoter score. You can also measure coaching activity by employee and manager. The correlation of employee engagement to attainment and results is a great way to profile top performers.

With metrics in hand and go-to-market clarity, the sales processes can be defined to create more consistency in coaching, selling, closing, and forecasting.

Sales Motions

Enablement professionals must lean into the sales processes and be a partner to sales operations and sales leaders. Who champions and sponsors the sales processes differs by company. What is for sure is that the vice president of sales is the ultimate executive sponsor of the processes, templates, and cadence.

It is up to you, the enablement professional, to wrestle down the vice president of sales, and any other stakeholders, to choose and customize the sales process. It is up to you to get the sales methodology codified in a sales system of record. The manager enablement and reinforcement training must be built on an agreed-upon sales process. In addition to the sales methodology, you need to look at quarterly business reviews, territory planning, pipeline reviews, deal reviews, and account-planning processes, too.

When processes aren't documented and communicated, expectations are not fully understood and embraced. The result is an organization that is not aligned, and key performance metrics are missed.

Choosing a Sales Methodology

Choosing a sales methodology is one of the most important decisions a company and vice president of sales can make to execute a successful go-to-market. A sales methodology is invaluable to grow predictable revenue faster by aligning sales and marketing, training sales professionals, executing deals consistently, and making this part of the sales culture.

Every company should have a documented sales methodology that's understood by each customer-facing employee, part of training/onboarding, and reinforced by front-line managers and VPs. I believe all established methodologies are created equal, and they are all great. Pick one (Selling Through Curiosity™, Target Account Selling, MEDDIC, The Challenger Sale, Value Selling, SPIN Selling, SNAP Selling, Miller Heiman, etc.) and make it your own.

Some leaders take a bit of each one and create their own. That's a good strategy too. It needs to map to your business values and go-to-market. The customization of a sales methodology is one of the key factors to make it stick and see business results.

The foundation of a sales methodology is the sales stages to follow and the sales-process questions to answer at each stage of the sales process. Everything flows from the stages and process. A typical set of stages for a technology company selling business-to-business (B2B) software is—

- Step 1: Qualification
- Step 2: Discovery
- Step 3: Demo/Trial
- Step 4: Mutual Plan
- Step 5: Proposal

Some companies add a couple more steps, and others shorten some steps. The name of the stages should map to the business. You'll find that most methodologies have a set of steps and questions. Review them and make sure they map to your values and culture.

Here are five operational questions to consider when selecting a sales methodology.

Question #1: How detailed are the coaching and input questions?

The sales methodology should have a list of questions that are a guide for a salesperson to answer during their sales pursuits. The questions should map to the company's go-to-market and take into consideration the buyer's journey.

Here are a few sales coaching questions that are thought provoking and great for running constructive deal conversations:

- How was the compelling event validated with top executives?
- How was value quantified and documented?
- How did we build relationships with our champion, executive sponsor, and influencers?
- What was known about the decision-making process?
- How were mutual plan expectations communicated and executed?

The aim of these questions is to give you and your team a framework to have a constructive sales coaching conversation in one-on-ones and team huddles.

Question #2: How does the methodology work with a sales automation system?

A methodology should come to life in a sales system like Salesforce CRM or Microsoft Dynamics. There are many different sales systems in the market. Choose one that maps to your business and will grow with you as you scale up your team.

Question #3: What do the reporting and forecasting processes look like?

The sales methodology should be reinforced by managers and leaders. Weekly reporting, one-on-ones, and business reviews should be informed by the data in the system. The conversations that happen should be based on the data that is being presented in the reports and forecast.

Question #4: How effective are the sales tools at building scale?

Create tools that reinforce the sales methodology. Educate product managers and product marketers about your sales methodology so they can create tools that are relevant and aligned with the sales methodology.

Question #5: What reinforcement training and onboarding tools are provided?

Create training that reinforces best practices and sales methodology learning outcomes. The training should be action oriented and include a dialogue about real deals. It's a great best practice to introduce the sales methodology early in the onboarding journey of new hires. Include deal-win stories that map to how your teams successfully executed the methodology.

There is a lot to do to choose, create, and execute following a sales methodology. I'll say it again and again: Choose one, and then customize it to your business to deliver the results you need to grow your business in a scalable and repeatable fashion.

Measure Sales Activities

There's a shortage of people who have the discipline to measure sales activity daily, weekly, and monthly. This happens because enablement professionals haven't done a great job explicitly communicating the right sales activity metrics and why they're important. Across the board (yes, I'm generalizing), we're not effectively connecting sales activity to revenue outcomes. We don't share expectations with our teams. It's time to realize that we can share our frustrations with our teams, or we can hold ourselves accountable.

Ask yourself what you have done to define, document, communicate, coach, measure, and celebrate the most important sales activities that are proven to close more deals in your business.

It's amazing to me how many sales leaders don't have the answers to foundational questions like the following: How many calls are my teams making a week? How many discovery meetings are happening each week? How many executive presentations are we doing each month?

Activity-Based Alignment

Inspired by Nick Sarles, former vice president of sales at SalesHood, our executive team spent time together looking at our historical deal data. We came up with our own sales activity metrics. We codified what we did to win and how we won. Tools and coaching were also created and shared to reinforce the activities. Nick also instituted a more disciplined way to execute our sales pursuits.

He recorded a weekly video broadcast that tallied the week's activities and reinforced our repeatable sales playbook. Nick's videos drove up the competitive spirit, too. Everyone in the company watched the videos and appreciated the visibility to the health of the business.

If you don't have your own sales activities documented and communicated, I encourage you to invest the time getting your list done. It'll give you more predictability and forecast accuracy. You'll also quickly know who is doing what on your teams. Data doesn't lie, and when you measure daily, weekly, and monthly activities, everything is open and transparent.

Sample Sales Activity Metrics

All too often, folks create a sales process but forget to get specific about sales activity metrics. For example, we see discovery as a step or a box on a sales process map. What we don't often see is the evidence to verify that a discovery call was completed. A good activity to track would be discovery call summaries that are written and shared with customers. These can easily be documented and tracked using any sales system.

More examples of metrics: number of demonstrations, number of meetings with executive sponsors and decision makers, number of proposals submitted, number of mutual plans shared, and number of order forms submitted. When you create your own list, look for proven activities that can be verified with evidence.

Build Discipline

Here are the steps required to build sales activity metrics discipline:

1. **Define Activities:** Look at the data and come up with a short list of sales activities that represent best practices. These are the activities that need to happen to win.

2. **Document Activities and Expectations:** Write down the sales activity metrics including expectations around the number of activities per deal, per day, per week, and per month.

3. **Communicate:** Don't wait. Tell your team sooner than later. Communicate often.

4. **Coach Your Team:** Make sure your team understands the activities and knows the steps to complete each one. Create tools and templates to keep your people focused on execution.

5. **Measure Activity:** Track accomplishments using whatever tool makes the most sense to you. Share leaderboards.

6. **Celebrate Successes:** As the activity increases, share stories and wins. Have teams highlight accomplishments, referencing the benefits of the sales activities executed.

7. **Iterate Activities:** Learn from the progress you're seeing (and not seeing), and make changes to the activities and expectations. Base decisions and updates on what's working and what's not.

We can't expect our teams to have the right quality and quantity of sales activities unless we invest the time to define, document, communicate, coach, measure, and celebrate a proven list of sales activities.

Sales Planning

As we begin executing our go-to-market, sales strategy and sales planning become increasingly more important. Planning takes many forms, from sales plans for sales leaders, and product plans for product managers, to territory plans for salespeople and sales managers. We will focus on territory planning since it is never quite done right.

Territory Planning

The goal of territory planning is to motivate your teams to prospect and self-source more pipeline. You need to help your sellers be more strategic about how and where they spend their time in their territories. I believe there's nothing better than old-school, back-to-basics territory planning and prospecting.

Think about what would happen if every salesperson documented their own territory plan and then video recorded a short and thoughtful five-minute version of it. Turn territory planning into an illuminating experience for your sales teams by making everyone part of the process and accountable for results. I believe quota-carrying sales executives need to own their self-sourcing pipeline.

Here are the secrets to making territory planning and prospecting a revenue-generating peer activity that is appreciated instead of criticized:

- Have vision and leadership to make it part of the sales culture.
- Make territory plans relevant, short, and accessible to share best practices.

• Do territory planning quarterly or monthly.

Companies that embrace the idea of video recording territory planning on a regular basis—with peer reviews—see tremendous increases in self-sourced pipeline and improvements in new-hire time to ramp. Think about it. Imagine if every new hire had access to stack-ranked video recordings of territory plans grouped by tenure. What would happen to your team's time-to-first-deal and time-to-ramp metrics?

The power and value of crowdsourcing is incredible. We all know that some of us are great at planning and others aren't. Making territory planning a team sport is a chance to get everyone to learn how to plan like those who do it best.

It takes vision to turn crowdsourcing territory plans into culture. It takes work to align teams on expectations. It takes discipline to make it stick.

Here are the basics of a territory plan proven to create pipeline and generate revenue fast. Make the plan relevant, short, and accessible. Share a territory-planning template that's relevant and short. Document the facts of the territory and goals in the first slide. Next, have your salespeople turn the territory plan into a business review by asking—

• What's my quota?
• What's my quota stretch goal?
• What's my closed business YTD?
• What's my gap?
• How much pipeline do I have today?
• What's my pipeline gap?
• What are my goals for the year?

Then move into top accounts. On the second slide, list out the names of the top accounts and explain why they are chosen (e.g., relationships, industry fit, target profile). For each, in one sentence, be clear and focused on the outreach strategy.

On a third slide, create an opportunity map, and make sure opportunity plans are thorough. Having a plan in place doesn't take much effort. What's the compelling event? Why now? What's the strategy to engage with a champion and economic buyer? What's the mutual success plan? Why now? We're not doing deep, detailed reviews.

Finally, for the last slide, close out with strategies to build pipeline.

Given that the template is short, forward-thinking leaders can build monthly and quarterly territory-planning cadence. The short plans get sellers to focus on strategy and execution instead of spending too much time filling out slides that aren't relevant. You want to see more sellers take the time to be thoughtful about their plan and business.

What I love most about this process is getting everyone to limit their territory planning to five minutes. Less is more. Fewer slides and fewer words is hard. We've learned when territory-planning video recordings are five minutes or less (and accessible), sellers will invest the time to watch up to fifteen peer territory plans. Let's push ourselves to get out of our comfort zone and answer the question, What do we have to do to achieve greatness?

ACCOUNT PLANNING

The same principles can be applied to account planning, which is another part of sales planning. Account planning isn't something you need to do with every account you're selling to or in every segment. For example, you're unlikely to drive a strategic account-planning program in your small business segments. On the bigger accounts, though, this is a mandatory practice. Many different processes out there can help align your sales teams and shape the right behaviors. While all the account-planning methodologies vary a bit, fundamentally they are grounded in similar principles. Account planning should include the following process steps:

1. Do research.
2. Build department or business-unit maps.
3. Build a political-influence map.
4. Create an account-based strategy.
5. Create a team-based action list.
6. Meet regularly as a team to review account strategies and progress.
7. Convert strategies into qualified opportunities.

Sales Planning Best Practices

I was working with a company to help roll out territory planning and account planning to their teams. We needed a way to make the activity relevant to everyone regardless of performance and tenure. We decided to create a three-level territory-planning initiative based on tenure. We outlined expectations and goals based on each salesperson's length of time in their role. We benchmarked their performance by looking at historical data like win rates, deal sizes, and pipeline generation. We asked each salesperson to create a territory plan and account plan. What we did that was unique was vary the scope of effort depending on the tenure. Each group completed relevant plans. The teams appreciated the exercise because it was personalized to them.

The newer salespeople, rookies, recorded territory plans focused on building pipeline and planning their business. The salespeople with a year or two under their belts were focused on opportunity planning because they had already invested the time to build their territory and pipeline and had deals in play. The more seasoned sales professionals were focused on just one or two accounts, and they went deep on account planning. We used benchmark data to find the top performers and share best practices.

With these best practices in hand, we could now work toward creating quarterly business reviews that were more collaborative and efficient.

Quarterly Business Reviews

It's no secret that most quarterly business reviews (QBRs) aren't well managed because they lack structure and engagement. Usually what happens is a manager sends out a QBR slide template used in a previous job. The team races to get it done with each person presenting their plan. The QBR turns into a glorified one-on-one coaching session between the manager and rep because everyone else in the room is updating or thinking about their plan. Most check out when it's not their turn. And it gets worse: There's no way to institutionalize the knowledge and experiences from preview QBRs.

Imagine what would happen if you had a library of previously submitted QBR plans with commentary and reviews sorted by rep tenure.

I'm confident if sales managers focus on making QBRs more collaborative and engaging, we'd realize better attainment and more best-practice sharing. The aim of the QBR is to create a plan that's going to get you to your commit and crush your number.

QUARTERLY BUSINESS REVIEW TEMPLATE

Here's a proven template and QBR meeting flow for sales managers to use with their teams.

Section 1: Sales Plan Activity

This section identifies priorities for the upcoming quarter. Get everyone on the team to answer the following questions:

1. What five opportunities are you most confident will close this quarter?

2. How much pipeline do you need to generate to hit your commit?

3. What are your personal development goals for the quarter?

Section 2: Big Deal Reviews

Systematically dive into top deals. Have teams give feedback and "score" deal review strategies. Here's a proven list of deal review questions:

1. What's the customer's current situation?

2. What are the customer's top problems and issues?

3. What are the financial impacts of the issues?

4. What are their ideals? What will their future look like if they solve these challenges?

5. What's the executive alignment strategy? How is it aligning with our champion, economic buyer, and influencers?

6. What's the company's compelling event?

7. What's the decision-making process? Who is involved? What are the evaluation criteria?

8. What are the quantifiable benefits of moving forward with a solution?

9. What's the competitive strategy? Who are we competing with, and how are we crushing the competition?

10. What are your next steps? What's your mutual plan?

Section 3: Loss Reviews

Review top losses from the previous quarter. Here are some questions to use when doing a competitive loss review with your team:

1. Why did you lose?

2. What would your customer say about why you lost?

3. What can you do to turn this deal around in the future?

Section 4: Win Reviews

Let's learn from our wins. Use this time to celebrate deal wins. Here are some best-practice deal-win questions:

1. Why did we win?
2. What business value did we create for our prospect?
3. How did we win?
4. What objections did you face during the evaluation, and how did we overcome them?
5. What did you learn from this win that will influence future deals?

Section 5: Prospecting Plan

Building pipeline is the key to closing deals. As our pipeline grows and we work more deals, the time we have to develop future pipeline decreases.

Use this section to plan out where you are going to dedicate your time to ensure pipeline growth is consistent.

Here are the questions to have teams answer:

1. Identify your ten priority accounts for the quarter.
2. Within these accounts, who are you going to target? Who is the economic buyer to target?
3. What's your value pitch in two or three sentences?
4. Identify one customer story that you will leverage to pique curiosity in the above accounts.
5. What are the key points from the above customer story that will resonate with your prospect accounts?
6. Share your outbound prospecting cadence.

Section 6: Support

Use this section to surface any challenges, obstacles, questions and/or comments. Give teams a chance to openly ask about support and/or questions they have.

Section 7: Action Items

Centralize and prioritize team action items to keep your teams focused and accountable.

Run your quarterly business reviews the right way and see—

- Better manager coaching
- More best-practice sharing
- Peer mentoring
- Higher attainment

Using Data to Drive an Executive Conversation

Now that you have a clearer understanding of the metrics that matter, you're better prepared to have data-driven enablement conversations to drive your enablement strategies and tactics. Every enablement strategy meeting should start with a review of the metrics. Have the data handy, and be ready to look at attainment and productivity results by team. You should even come prepared with a printout for everyone to review and discuss together. Having this data will elevate your game.

Keep it simple. An easy-to-read yet comprehensive one-slide summary table will suffice. Showing the year-over-year change is great to do as well and gives good context. Do not let the finance and operations team share summary slides that are difficult to understand and use. Push your peers to simplify the data. If you are still not getting the right information, walk into the office of your chief revenue officer or your chief executive officer and let them know you are not able to do your job because you do not have all the information you need to make decisions. Here are some of my lessons learned to engage the C-suite and earn your seat at the table:

- Be organized.
- Be strategic.
- Have a plan.
- Show the data.
- Clarify expected outcomes.
- Be clear on timelines.

Once you follow these guidelines, you can start reaping the benefits of mastering the data and promoting the results; you'll get universal buy-in for your sales enablement initiatives.

ROI and Budgets

Armed with data, budget and resource discussions are made easier. Enablement is all about math: the math to calculate the cost-benefit analysis of resource allocation. Equipped with these solid metrics, you can tie your sales enablement efforts to results in the field. This not only impacts revenue attainment, but it also boosts your ability to justify the right budget for sales enablement programs.

I was first introduced to this idea back in my early days at Salesforce. We looked at spreadsheets of attainment, win rates, and ramp times of the global sales organization. We made sure we were always making the right enablement bets. We calculated the ROI on every enablement resource and initiative. The calculation was based on revenue impact and was closely tied to attainment by region. We also created teams of shared services that would support sales teams in their sales pursuits. We were focused on increasing attainment and looking for ways to improve win rates, reduce sales-cycle time, increase deal sizes, and increase customer-facing selling time. It sounds almost impossible to be able to accomplish all the above at the same time.

One day at Salesforce we noticed a lot of inbound requests from our sales teams to help with business case development. The market was maturing, and customers were beginning to ask for help to build financial justifications. We had an analyst focus on helping the sales teams full time. We noticed trends. Every time we worked on a business case collaboratively with a customer, we won the deal. We noticed win rates skyrocketing, resulting in higher attainment. We also noticed that salespeople spent less time on the administration and calculations of business cases and more time selling. It was the trifecta of enablement multipliers. After running this for six months and measuring the impact, I went back to Linda and Frank and made an argument for a team of business case specialists. We calculated and justified the incremental based on improvements in attainment and win rates. The math was simple and straightforward.

Plans by Role

As a company's go-to-market matures, the enablement complexities increase. A one-size-fits-all approach to enablement will not work and will result in bad sales enablement. A helpful planning exercise to do in partnership with leadership is the following: Make a list of all the employee and partner roles in your company. For each role, list the tools and processes they need to be successful. Include a metric for each one. Identify the assessment required to check competence. Document the list. Share it with stakeholders. Get alignment of what tools and content need to be created.

The enablement planning matrix will become the contract that exists between teams that need to work together to achieve go-to-market goals. Your stakeholders, and specifically your individual employees, will appreciate the thoughtfulness of a plan that is tailored to their role and success criteria.

KEY TAKEAWAYS

With hundreds of sales enablement tools available in the sales technology stack and so many competing priorities, sales enablement leaders are struggling to figure out where to focus and what to do next. CROs have priorities. CMOs are asking for access and more product enablement. Sales managers are looking for answers. Salespeople are hungry for less noise.

Let's proclaim a sales attainment manifesto to help us collectively prioritize where we spend time:

- Have a data mindset, and don't be afraid to get the data.
- Get the data.

- Correlate coaching activity and enablement initiatives with attainment data.

- Work closely with sales operations to get this data. With the data correlated and hooked between data sources, it's finally possible to see what is working and what is not.

Anytime your sales enablement program lifts your team's ability to hit quota, top line will be massively impacted. Sales enablement and a maniacal focus on sales attainment data is the path to success.

Chapter 7

Learning

When was the last time you watched the movie *Ferris Bueller's Day Off*? My family and I watched the movie on New Year's Eve in 2017. Our kids at the time were ten and almost eight. The film stars Matthew Broderick as Ferris Bueller, a high school slacker who spends a day off from school with a couple friends having fun in Chicago. One of the first scenes of the movie takes place in a classroom setting. A teacher, in a dry and monotonous voice, asks the class questions in a nonengaging manner. The kids' faces show boredom and blank stares. One student stares into space, blowing a bubble-gum balloon. No one wants to be there.

My kids thought the scene was funny. They were hysterical. They kept looking at each other, smiling and laughing. What was the private joke I was missing? They said that this way of learning was funny. Having a teacher ask rhetorical questions in a nonengaging way, basically reading from a textbook, is not how children expect to learn today.

In a world of interactive learning models, iPads, devices, whiteboards, storytelling, and collaboration, passive learning seems ancient to my children. They are lucky to have great teachers who make learning fun and engaging.

Today, we expect engaging, interactive, fun, thought-provoking, and immersive learning. Some call this a flipped classroom. Wikipedia explains the flipped classroom like this:

> Flipped classroom is an instructional strategy and a type of blended learning that reverses the traditional learning environment by delivering instructional content, often online, outside of the classroom. It moves activities, including those that may have traditionally been considered homework, into the classroom. In a flipped classroom, students watch online lectures, collaborate in online discussions, or carry out research at home and engage in concepts in the classroom with the guidance of a mentor.[7]

As enablement professionals, we are responsible for executing high-impact training. We spend days and months building curriculum. We work with our subject-matter experts to create training content. We spend weeks managing project plans having to create training content, review it, test it, validate it, and produce it. We do all this work and then, once the training is done, we wonder why we have not changed the mindset and behavior of our people. We wonder why we are not seeing the results we expect. It gets worse. Many researchers claim that up to 90 percent of what is taught is forgotten in less than a week. We spend so much money and resources, and we still do not see the desired results.

In this chapter, we explore the principles of active learning,

---

7   "Flipped Classroom," Wikipedia.com, https://en.wikipedia.org/wiki/Flipped_classroom, accessed April 2018.

including how to create flipped classrooms in corporations to overcome learning and retention issues. We will review examples of active learning to increase learning outcomes to deliver better product training, skills training, assessments, social learning, coaching, and onboarding.

Enabling with Video Is Better

During one of my client visits in New York, I met up with my friend Chris Mezzatesta, chief revenue officer at Newsela. When Chris introduced me to his team, I felt a warm welcome. Everyone thanked me for being a part of their success. The gratitude came from top-performing sales execs, newly hired employees, and even the CEO. I was humbled.

I asked Chris what his secret was to success. He said that he and his teams are super disciplined about capturing company moments using video. They record every meeting and every all-hands call and publish it for current and future hires. Video helps companies like Newsela scale their learning initiatives and make their training more impactful.

Videos will not entirely replace face-to-face interactions, but they make our time together more productive. Videos should be informal. I am not talking about a marketing video that lives on a website. The kind of videos I am referring to here are the videos of someone sitting at their desk. I love seeing executives do a personal broadcast video from their home or office. It is OK to have pauses in a video and even the occasional "um" and "oh." It is real life. We are using video to capture real life as best we can. We will never remove the need for real human interaction.

Cost Savings

Companies spend an estimated more than three hundred billion a year on corporate training. We know how much it costs to fly teams to central locations to sit through training and workshops. How often do you hear: "The event was good, but most of what was covered could have been done over video"? How much money is wasted annually just on travel and entertainment expenses that could be avoided with more on-demand training?

Increased Knowledge

Knowledge retention from webinars, offsites, or conferences is quite low. Video is a way to modernize these practices by serving up short, accessible videos on demand for teams to watch and review on their own time before and after events. It also serves as a way to capture knowledge by asking teams to answer questions and share video updates. Technology is available to make this happen at scale, including capture, transcription, and full search.

Video is a proven way to scale peer-to-peer best-practice sharing. Silos come down with corporate video storytelling, and knowledge sharing is accelerated. Video is the way for product managers to get internal and external teams up to speed fast on new product releases, campaigns, and launches. Video becomes the ultimate in capturing and cross-pollinating ideas and feedback from virtual and distributed teams.

Increased Data

Video helps us know what content is being consumed by whom and what content is not valued. The power of video is that we know who watched our videos and for how long. The analytics is there to answer the content-effectiveness questions in real time. The challenge we face is we do not fully understand how to effectively use video in our jobs, when to best use video, and what to use the videos for after we have them.

Human Connection

Video is powerful because, if done right, it is authentic, fast, efficient, memorable, scalable, personal, and repeatable. What I am talking about here is the kind of video that a real person records about their own personal experience. The kind of video that people know won't be shared on YouTube. These kinds of videos are the moments and the knowledge we want to help enable companies to capture. Video helps put humanity back into team communications.

When you see an authentic video, you get a glimpse into who a person really is by looking in their eyes and seeing their body language. You can tell a lot about their intent. Look in their eyes and ask yourself how much they are owning the content, or are they reading?

Healthy Competition Accelerates Learning

Videos that are recorded and open for viewing create a positive competitive environment. Who does not want to look great in front of their peers? Who will not put their best foot forward? My experience and the data show us that individuals and managers will step up and do the best work of their lives. The act of sharing a video to a team of peers that represents work goals and accomplishments will result in great outcomes. It is similar to hitting the gym. Doing the work and putting time in at the gym or on a treadmill or the pavement will yield positive outcomes. The same is true in a professional setting.

I was once asked to review a team's quarterly plans. They missed their team targets. The department leader called me up to ask for some help. What can we do to motivate the team? How can we get them to exceed their goals in the new quarter? We decided to have them make a video. We came up with a set of goals and walked the team through their team goals. After asking about obstacles and challenges, we removed all of them and then gave them a task. We asked them to take the plan template and record their plan. What happened next was amazing.

Everyone on the team put their heart and soul into the exercise. They recorded their videos, and as the videos came in, they became more intense. The team got energy from each other. One of the last videos to come in was recorded at three in the morning. I watched it, and I knew that person was going to exceed their goals, and they did. The salesperson was filled with purpose and intent. You could tell by looking at the body language, expressions, and hand gestures. He was carefully thinking through every word he was saying. Every word and sentence was calculated. He looked like an athlete ready to be on the field for the big game, and no one was going to come between this person and winning.

Managers are able to quickly see how their team is doing. They form an opinion from day one about how much coaching will be required to get this new hire productive and integrated.

Video storytelling is a powerful way to enable teams to share knowledge and be successful, and it is powerful for every role in a corporation. Some are faster to adopt than others. Salespeople and customer-facing employees are naturally the early adopters. The best advice is to drive a video communication and enablement strategy from the top. Getting leaders to share their stories first in a nonformal way gets everyone motivated to share. The informality of a video lowers the barriers to entry for employees. Make videos personal, relevant, and accessible to realize the full benefits of cross-team knowledge sharing.

The Science of Learning and Reinforcement

I always somehow knew that people retained more knowledge by doing. You learn a new skill, and you practice it until you know it. I applied this theory to business. One day I got curious and wondered if there was any research or science behind my hypothesis.

Hermann Ebbinghaus was a German psychologist "who pioneered the experimental study of memory and is known for his discovery of the forgetting curve and the spacing effect. He was also the first person to describe the learning curve."[8] His central hypothesis states that increased learning comes from greater experience, or the more someone does something, the better they get at it. Learning will happen over time and over a series of actions completed over and over. Repetition works to help increase learning.

As enablement professionals, we need to apply these principles to all our learning programs. We need to create a

---

8   "Hermann Ebbinghaus," Wikipedia.com, https://en.wikipedia.org/wiki/ Hermann_Ebbinghaus, accessed April 2018.

culture where learning is ongoing and repetitive. We want to teach our salespeople and managers to apply learning to the real deal to accelerate results. This learning technique is called active learning.

I uncovered another piece of research on learning retention. The Learning Pyramid was created by the National Training Laboratories in Bethel, Maine.[9] It states that our learning retention is directly related to the degree of active learning. It is an effective anchor to drive the principle of an enablement program grounded in active-learning principles. Real learning comes from making mistakes. And mistakes come from applying the learning to real-life scenarios.

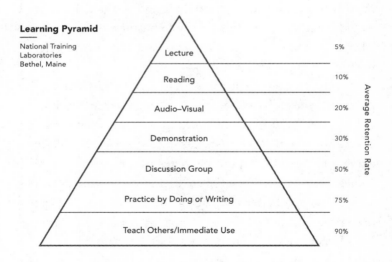

Figure 7.1: Learning Pyramid

---

9   NTL Institute for Applied Behavioral Science, Alexandria, Virginia.

Adopting Active-Learning Techniques

Students show they have mastered subjects when they can verbalize in their own words what something means. They learn faster and apply things better when they practice, make mistakes, and get feedback. The fastest way to get people to learn a topic is to make them part of the learning process and to have them own their learning outcomes.

This active learning occurs when a person takes control of their learning experience. Active learning is realized through testing, assessments, storytelling, practice drills, and role-playing. Social learning accelerates the outcomes of active learning too, when experienced peers give each other feedback and coaching. Passive learning is through lecture. We will not be discussing the merits of lecture-based learning. Lectures fail to achieve results unless they are coupled with active learning.

We need to teach people in different ways for many reasons. People consume content and learn differently. Some people like to consume content by reading. Other people like to learn by watching videos. Some people prefer to collaborate and share ideas as a method of learning. For some, learning is a solo sport, and for others it's a group dynamic that helps optimize learning outcomes. Others prefer to put pen to paper and learn by writing. Some topics have more optimal ways of learning than others. Product training can be accomplished with a knowledge-check test. Let us review some of the more effective active-learning and assessment methods that work well for product training and skills training. These are great building blocks to custom design learning to meet your needs.

Icebreaker

The icebreaker method is intended to help people get to know each other and let their guards down. It is great to do at the beginning of a day-long training event or a virtual session. It is how most meetings should start when people are meeting for the first time. I like having people introduce themselves and share a fun fact about themselves. The ultimate icebreaker conversation starter is the "If you really knew me, you'd know that . . ." question asked at parties. Everyone introduces themselves and completes the sentence.

Other great icebreaker questions are—

- What is your role, and how long have you been at the company?
- What are you looking to accomplish from this training or event?
- What is your name, and what city are you from?
- What is your favorite band and why? What is the first music concert you attended?
- What is your favorite movie and why?
- What's your personal story?

Team Discussion

The next mode of active learning is to answer a question that maps to a specific topic. This type of active learning is called team discussion. Once you get into a topic, slow the curriculum down and have your students answer a question or share an experience to promote team discussion. Your teams should write down an answer on a piece of paper or key an answer into a system. The pen-to-paper method of learning is very powerful. At the right point in your content and curriculum, have everyone sitting at tables or in their chairs write down their answers to a given question. If you have tables of eight to ten people, have everyone at a table share their answers, one by one. This is collaborative and inclusive learning. Each table can then share their conclusions and the lessons they learned. You can also pair people off and have person A share, then person B.

The team discussion is a great way to explore how people are internalizing the training. It is a great way to test knowledge in a non-testing way. It lets people start applying the topic to their jobs and workflow.

Role Play

Another active learning method is role play. With role-play exercises, teams are given a scenario, and they respond to the scenario. For salespeople, a good role play to practice is how to handle a typical customer objection. For customer support people, a good role play is to practice handling a tough customer conversation. A scenario is given with detailed instruction and then everyone responds to the scenario.

The role play can be handled in person in a classroom setting or online with video recordings. Ideal role-play exercises are optimized when the scope of the work takes less than five to ten minutes to optimize engagement. The power of the role play is to drive peer-to-peer feedback and learning from each other.

Create a library of scenario-based role-play exercises to help people be better prepared for conversations and tasks they will be performing in their day-to-day jobs. Documenting role-play scenarios and creating a forum and space to role-play is the job of enablers.

Stand and Deliver

Another method of active learning is stand and deliver. The way this learning method works is to have students prepare a presentation that they then deliver before a team. The presentation can be an elevator pitch, a product demonstration, an executive presentation, and so on. It can be short or long depending on the goals.

I was speaking with Roque Versace, a well-respected sales leader and friend, and he shared with me that the stand and deliver method was the best way to ensure that sales professionals learn. "Get up and pitch," he said, "whether it be corporate messaging, the product value proposition for a particular industry, competitive handles, elevator pitches—whatever it is you want a rep to know.

"Nothing delivers as well as an employee doing a live pitch. They often kick and scream, but after the exercise, the feedback is that the stand and deliver exercises were the most helpful." The pressure of being seen by their peers and the competitiveness of sales professionals heightens their senses and brings out the best in them. Technology makes stand and deliver cost effective and scalable. A company can leverage video, mobile, and social on a global scale—without flying everyone in—to make sure their reps have learned what they need to learn to be successful. The stand and deliver active-learning method works great for new-hire onboarding, product launches, and sales kickoff events.

Building a culture where stand and deliver happens often is incredibly valuable in improving employee productivity and knowledge sharing. There are many ways to do stand and deliver to improve learning outcomes. Managers have their teams do presentations in one-on-ones and in team huddles.

Departments run stand and deliver during team offsites or in person. Department leaders spot-check stand and delivers when they travel and visit teams. Stand and deliver works best when managers and employees practice authentic coaching and feedback.

Incorporate Testing

Another method of active learning is doing knowledge quizzes. Testing is a great way to capture immediate knowledge readiness. It is our job to know what our teams need to practice so they can be the best at what they do. Testing and knowledge checks are a great way to reinforce learning, assess where we stand, and determine who on our teams understands the concepts and can apply them effectively in their jobs. Testing is done through questions and answers of all types.

Testing can be in the form of an online or written test where students answer questions. The question types are true and false, pick the right answers, pick multiple right answers, and essay questions. All are good and complement a diverse active-learning program. Some enablement programs do too much testing. Some organizations test daily, weekly, and monthly. Technology makes it easy to automate the distribution and testing of questions and answers. Try not to fall into that trap. Keep learning and assessments fun and creative. Learning outcomes will be enhanced, and students will appreciate the range of content and learning assessments.

Social Learning and Peer Reviews

Two of my favorite methods of active learning are social learning and peer reviews. The learning pyramid confirms that people learn and retain the most when they are teaching others. An example of salespeople wanting to learn more and be better by sharing and peer reviewing comes from Sheevaun Thatcher. She was vice president of sales productivity at Host Analytics. She led the charge to improve rep confidence and competence around handling competitive positioning. The reps needed to quickly overcome their fears and be in a position to not let competitive objections defeat them. They sat with the leadership and recorded their top competitive objections. The videos were short and focused.

The results were eye-opening to Sheevaun and me. Everyone on her team was asked to watch the videos, and then they needed to be certified on one or more of those competitive objections. Over four days, on average their salespeople watched, recorded, and reviewed those videos at least forty-two times. Her people recorded their videos between five to seven times each. Repetition proved to be what the reps needed. They became ready in days, and they did it by boosting each other. Their pipeline skyrocketed by 27 percent in a week, and their competitive win rates improved by 42 percent.

Sheevaun and Host Analytics were looking to improve competitive win rates with peer-to-peer video challenges. The revenue outcome was clear and understood. The goals and missions were communicated and aligned. Sheevaun shared with me that "widespread understanding of the why is the sales enablement secret to driving behavior and results."

We saw similar results and engagement with many other companies. These stories and guiding principles both showcase the growing trend of sales professionals investing time to improve their skills by learning from each other.

Case Study: Reinforcing Product Training

One of the pieces of enablement excellence many companies skip is reinforcement. There are many flavors to reinforcement. Many believe knowledge checks test reinforcement. I will argue that applying the new skills and messages to real-life situations while collaborating with a team is the ultimate in reinforcement and is not done enough. Knowledge is more effectively consumed, shared, and retained in a team huddle.

A **huddle** is a way for teams to collaborate and share ideas. It is a proven way to help teams focus on key metrics like growing revenue and closing business. It is a way to connect priorities with content and with front-line manager coaching. While we're talking about sales coaching, this practice is a good one for non-sales managers to follow, too.

In sales, teams come together and huddle around a deal or a product launch. They share what they know, and they ask each other questions. Great managers facilitate dialogue that is about knowledge sharing.

Bob Kruzner, director of enablement from ServiceMax, shared with me some of the challenges he had with a product release. ServiceMax came out with three new product offerings. These products were strategic and material to growing the business and differentiating against the competition in pursuits with new customers and existing customers. They had a clear vision of how they wanted their teams to sell these products. Bob brought marketing and subject-matter experts together to build the Product Huddle.

They released huddles that walked their managers and sales teams through the new product offerings. They created consistency around how they wanted their teams to learn and share best practices. They used videos to communicate positioning, a demonstration of the product features, quizzes, and Q&A modules covering typical objections. Bob created the Huddle to get the best practice in the hands of his teams, but more importantly he wanted his managers to facilitate conversation with their teams on the top objections. That is the ultimate in coaching and knowledge sharing.

Bob also had the teams engage with the product playbook to share how they would apply the product and content to active deals in their pipeline. Each team member shared a deal and gave others feedback. Collaborative discussions were created along with a practice pitch applying the product to that deal. The Huddle also included all the needed tools and assets that are helpful for sales teams.

The results were amazing. The teams were engaged. The teams were watching content and engaging with content in a whole new way that improved knowledge, tracked effectiveness, and boosted results. They are now closing bigger deals because the teams are collaborating to share best practices.

Launch Initiatives with Managers First

Sales enablement initiatives have a high degree of success when we ensure that front-line managers get the information first and are on message. Employee engagement is directly correlated to manager engagement. This is why we must first get managers aligned and then the entire team.

When managers are trained and certified first, their team's activities are 100 percent complete. The result is higher attainment. When a company rolls out a new pitch and managers go first, everyone gets certified faster and better. Higher sales attainment follows.

The data shows that when managers go first, the rest of the team follows. Knowing this, I was working with Chris Harrington, president from Domo. He appreciated the importance of his managers completing the messaging certification first. He needed to improve win rates fast, and to do that he needed to get his entire company speaking the same brand and company message. They needed to be able to quickly change the conversation to focus on customer-use cases and value. Chris went first and recorded his pitch from his Tesla right after a dentist appointment because he wanted his managers to go next. Chris wanted the "sales enablement party" to be started when his sales and services teams recorded their pitch certifications. He witnessed 100 percent completion by managers and 100 percent completion by his sales and services teams. It was the beginning of their sales transformation, and their results were incredible. They increased attainment by 300 percent and then also did another fund raise with a higher valuation.

I cannot overstate the importance of managers going first. There is a direct performance correlation between team quota attainment and a manager doing their pitch first. The data shows that salespeople will first go see their manager's pitch. They want to see how their manager does it. If a manager does one, the entire team will do one. If the entire team does one, the entire team will invest the time to score each other. Performance will improve. If the manager does not do one, all the collaboration and social learning is diminished.

Consider the number of learning touches that happens in a single productivity initiative led by managers going first. With a team of eight to ten individuals, if a manager goes first, then each member of the team will watch their manager's presentation. Each person will then practice their version five to seven times. After they share their version, they will watch everyone on the team deliver their own. They will most likely watch each one a few times. Everyone will help each other be better.

Onboarding

The process of training and onboarding salespeople and new employees is still broken. Even with all the technology and automation we have in the world, for many companies, sales attainment and new-hire ramp time are not improving. New hires at some B2B companies take over a year to start hitting quota. We see the average time to ramp a new rep to be over 270 days before using SalesHood and fewer than 90 days after using our technology. CSO Insights validates the number with 40.2 percent of their survey respondents reporting ramp-up time of greater than ten months. We also don't talk a lot about all the salespeople that don't make it. Those numbers are high too.

The reason for this industry-wide miss is we're not looking at onboarding as a journey. Rather, we look at it as an event at one point in time, like a boot camp that starts and ends during the employee's first week of work.

We're not highlighting top performer best practices. We're not providing structured learning paths and embracing learn-by-doing principles. We tend to miss the ever-so-important peer feedback and mentorship. We don't do enough expectation setting around practice and coaching. Last, and probably the most important, is that we don't do enough to get alignment and clarity around the performance metrics that matter at every step in the onboarding journey by role.

Getting sales teams performing better and faster is the way to quickly grow business. It's how we did it at Salesforce, and it's one of the most important initiatives for young startups. The first step to creating a scalable, revenue-generating sales onboarding plan is to align on metrics. We all want to front-end the process with metrics that help sales to focus on the right behaviors and actions. For example, we want to measure pipeline generated, time to first deal, and time to quota attainment. We should create onboarding that blends self-paced work with certifications, team-based exercises, and role plays. The following best-practice onboarding story will help you build learning paths that will reduce time to ramp and make you a revenue superstar contributor in your company.

The Telogis-Verizon Story

At our 2016 annual customer conference, Kelly Frey, vice president of marketing at Telogis, presented a talk on the importance of aligning marketing and sales to improve sales productivity. He talked about his journey and how he and his team, over time, created a lot of content and knowledge. He brought a great chart showing the considerable growth of content creation and content consumption month over month. We'd all like to show a similar chart when presenting our enablement results.

Kelly explained that what we were looking at was the collective knowledge created at Telogis. He explained that the content represented a lot of different types of knowledge from a variety of groups: marketing-generated content in the form of corporate presentations; content generated by product management and engineering in the form of product knowledge;

content generated by subject-matter experts from weekly company calls that are recorded and shared; user-generated content from individual contributors like salespeople; executive-generated content, including business plans and quarterly goals; and customer-generated content from customer interviews and stories. Kelly then said that the sum total of this content is what makes his company who they are. He said that it was bigger than their culture, that it was their secret sauce.

The metrics Kelly highlighted focused on attainment and time to revenue, the key performance indicators that are the biggest sign of success for Kelly and Telogis. "My ultimate key performance indicator at Telogis is to help sales sell bigger deals faster," he said. At Telogis, they improved time to first deal by 70 percent. They reduced the average number of days from 266 to 85. The business benefits are extremely positive and the dream of many enablement professionals.

Another metric that Kelly measured is the percentage of a cohort that achieved their first deal in six months. They went from zero to 70 percent. Their leadership team recognized how amazing this sales productivity number was to the company and ultimately to one of the factors that led to the acquisition by Verizon.

I love this quote from Kelly: "We could close deals faster and bigger than our competition." What sales leader, salesperson, sales manager, or chief executive officer does not want this too?

Telogis Onboarding Framework

I interviewed Kelly Frey, and we talked about the onboarding framework at Telogis. He shared that there is a four-week learning path for enterprise sales executives. These are experienced sales professionals, so the learning path needs to include an appropriate amount of learning, coaching, and best-practice sharing.

The first week is focused on "How We Win." The second week is themed around "What We Sell" with an emphasis on products and solutions. The third week, called "Who Do We Sell To," is focused on personas. Finally, the fourth week is focused on "How Do We Close." At the end of each week, there is a pitch contest to practice and reinforce learning. He also encourages his people to tell the company story in a one-minute elevator pitch.

The learning path includes both self-paced learning and group learning. The new hires are constantly evaluated and provided feedback and tips. The learning path is comprehensive and achievable with about seven hours of work a week over a month. Kelly said: "The learning path is a reasonable amount of time because our salespeople are hungry in the early days and eager to understand the products, verticals, competition, and success stories."

Company-Wide Onboarding

In 2017, we ran our third-annual SalesHood customer conference. We invited our customers to speak at our event. The topics ranged from sales operations and sales enablement to sales management. The agenda and conversation were shaping up nicely. One of our keynotes was a talk by Kamal Ahluwalia, the chief revenue officer, and Aaron Farley, head of enablement from Apttus. What struck me as different from previous sales talks was Kamal and Aaron's emphasis on enablement and learning being a company-wide initiative. Every single employee would go through new hire-training together, including twenty hours of prework and a boot camp, regardless of role. Training would be for everyone, not just salespeople.

New hires were asked to record their own company pitch presentation. Expectations were set that there needed to be some understanding of the value proposition. Apttus wanted everyone at their company to be on message and speaking the same language. They initially ran the all-employee corporate pitch certification as an experiment. The non-salespeople were nervous and anxious. Apttus challenged their new employees and got every employee to raise their game.

The long-term impact was far-reaching. Besides improvements in productivity, there were also implications to culture. Going forward, when employees were asked to do things, they were ready. Non-sales employees were appreciative and grateful. They thanked Aaron for helping them understand how their jobs impacted the broader company health. One of my favorite quotes from Aaron's talk is "Apttus helps its employees more confidently talk about what they do and be able to sit down with their mom and explain it too." That's powerful.

The Apttus story continues with company-wide enablement across every role and every employee. Kamal, now President at Eightfold.ai, has carried his conviction around enablement into his new venture and turned it into a foundation block—not something that's brought in later. We proved that enablement done right is a sought-after business strategy for every company, division, leader, and manager.

Onboarding Checklist

A thorough onboarding plan is developed to increase the likelihood of hitting quota much faster through enablement and onboarding. What goes into a 30-60-90-day sales onboarding plan? How should it be structured? How does peer mentoring play a part? How are managers engaged? How is the sales process introduced and learned? How often do check-ins happen? What are the right kinds of certifications?

As you think about your 30-60-90-day sales onboarding plan, here is a checklist you can use to onboard your sales teams:

1. Include ten to twenty hours of prework before joining an in-person boot camp.

2. Keep videos short and concise, using talking heads instead of slides as much as possible.

3. Organize the flow of content and exercises to map to the sales process.

4. Host check-ins weekly in the first thirty days and then every two weeks thereafter.

5. Keep managers engaged with regular updates and rep performance scorecards.

6. Create onboarding plans by employee role.

There is a lot you can automate with new-hire onboarding, and there are some parts that need human interaction. Make sure you are striking the right balance. Also, be sure to include the learning and content pillars proven to get teams up to speed and productive faster.

Company Story, Culture, and Values

Create a rich library of videos and stories that cover company story, culture, and values. I recommend asking senior executives and top performers to share their stories and experiences.

It's a great way to get people introduced to your company. This should happen at the beginning of the sales onboarding plan.

Customer Stories

Include examples of reference customers by industry, product, segment, and geography. Make the stories short and filled with memorable details salespeople can use in their prospecting and customer conversations. The customer stories will be inspirational and aspirational for new hires. It's always better when our new hires hear from our customers as well as hear what customer success looks like.

Sales Process

Map out exercises, discussions, role play, and teamwork around the sales process and sales stages. Sequence the stages in order, and stage exercises that are mapped to real account, prospect, and customer outreach. Having new hires go through the motions together with real accounts is the ideal way to do this. Here is a list of common stages and sales onboarding work that would be good for new hires to do as a group and with their managers and mentors:

- Stage 1: Research companies and contacts. Send emails.
- Stage 2: Write out qualification and discovery questions.
- Stage 3: Create a customized presentation and practice presenting. Get feedback from peers and manager.
- Stage 4: Create a proposal with pricing and solution details.
- Stage 5: Map out the procurement process for a real deal and prepare commercials.

Product Training

Provide product training in phases. Don't overwhelm and firehose your teams. Do product overviews and introductory videos. More hands-on training should come later. Focus on competence and confidence. You should target product fluency instead of expecting product mastery in the first few weeks. Put your subject-matter experts and product managers in front of the camera to share their product vision and story. They'll appreciate doing it once but not every time you hire new people.

Certifications and Assessment

Create short certifications and assessment that are mapped to the sales process and sales stages. These are also called stand and deliver exercises. Certify your team on the elevator pitch, the corporate overview, first meeting presentation, second meeting presentation, and all conversations that move deals through the buyer's journey. Objection handling is another common certification. Make certification relevant and as real to life as you can. Think about your new hire's journey and schedule the right certification at the right time. For example, don't certify someone on processing an order if you don't expect them to need to know that skill until several weeks after their start date.

Experts to Meet

Create lists of experts, executives, and top performers whom it would be helpful to meet. It takes a village, and building a network is the way to increase ramp time. While you can automate a lot of the onboarding, the human connection is important. Create time for new hires to meet experts in groups or in one-on-ones.

Call Shadowing

Curate mentorship and call shadowing. Make it mandatory that new hires reach out to as many sales peers as possible to call shadow. Put them on a schedule and hold them accountable. They should report back what they observed and how they'll apply the lessons learned in their own territory and deals. Their observations will be telling about what future coaching is required.

Call Coaching

After they've sat through their quota of shadow calls, salespeople should be shadowed as they graduate to leading their own customer calls. Focus on the fundamentals and make sure they are being curious and conducting discovery and relationship building the right way.

Check-ins

Keep a schedule of check-ins. Sixty minutes a week will go a long way in helping a new hire feel they have a support network around them, but check-ins are often overlooked. Give them an opportunity to ask questions and hear from their peers.

The sales onboarding plan's goal is to establish a clear set of expectations and actions for sales managers and reps to do together to hit quota faster.

Building Content

You don't have to feel as though you alone are responsible for building all the content. You can't do it alone. It takes a team. You need to engage all your subject-matter experts, product managers, sales managers, and leaders to build a rich library of crowdsourced content. Don't wait until boot camp to get your new hires introduced to deal-win stories, executive interviews, and top customer presentations. Crowdsource the stories and pitches and make them available to your teams the moment after they sign your offer letter. Engage subject-matter experts and product managers to use video to capture their knowledge and scale the distribution of it.

You're a lot closer than you think. Crowdsource deal wins. Crowdsource customer stories. Crowdsource top-performer territory plans, email templates, and account plans. Collate the top customer presentations from your top performers. Organize the content and make it available to your teams. Have a vision in mind and create a phased approach to content development that delivers value to new hires and the bottom line faster.

The goal with onboarding should be to help teams put points on the board as quickly as possible while reducing the need for long on-site boot camps. Those are expensive and aren't conducive for quality learning and retention. Start thinking about onboarding as a thirty-day virtual journey with prework, mentorship, and milestones instead of a one-week intensive boot camp experience.

Use new-hire onboarding to build a stand and deliver learning culture. Many companies put emphasis on a single stand and deliver certification event. That doesn't work well. Follow what the best companies do and create micro-certifications. Have salespeople stand and deliver simulated role plays for elevator pitches, customer storytelling, objection handling, and product demonstrations. Have the final stand and deliver certification be a customer presentation based on a real customer deal.

Make onboarding a company-wide activity with product managers and subject-matter experts creating content and managers and leaders coaching and mentoring.

Virtual Reality and Learning

We hosted a virtual reality experience in New York, and it opened my eyes to the future. It's amazing how far virtual reality has come. After trying out several virtual reality experiences, like walking through landscapes on this planet and abroad, walking the plank (and jumping), and then flying through the skies, I realized its power. As different experiences and scenarios presented themselves to me, I was asked to participate and go deeper and deeper. It took practice and role-playing to the next level for me. Did I mention I'm afraid of heights, yet I was willing to walk on a plank and jump off a building. What an amazing way to get over fears, uncertainty, and doubt.

The implications of these sort of experiences are tremendous for corporations, especially around training, coaching, and selling. We can leapfrog engagement and education hurdles by immersing our teams and customers into virtual reality role-play simulations. With virtual reality, we'll see salespeople practicing their pitch in a simulated boardroom and with customers raising objections in augmented conversations.

KEY TAKEAWAYS

It is easy to take the passive way of learning and not creatively come up with ways for employees to learn and share best practices. Be creative with your training content and learning exercises, and watch your people be creative with their learning.

- Integrate active-learning methods in training curriculum, such as icebreakers, storytelling, team discussions, role plays, and stand and deliver presentations.
- Embracing active-learning methods results in better learning retention and better business outcomes.
- Map learning outcomes with active learning methods.

Chapter 8

Communications

How we create, curate, and consume content in the corporate world is changing. In the past we trained with books and workshops, but now we utilize vignettes and videos. With these practical changes, so too have our assumptions about content consumption shifted. The content we are creating is inspired by a new generation of workers who expect information and answers to be delivered right here, right now.

In the great TED talk "How a Handful of Tech Companies Control Billions of Minds Every Day," Tristan Harris shared his perspective on how people are connecting with technologies like Facebook, Instagram, and Snapchat. He talked about the "race for attention" and the attention economy. Many of us use these social applications on a regular basis. As a society, we spend hours and hours a day watching videos, liking photos, wishing people virtual happy birthdays, and sharing pictures. Harris got me thinking about the implications of how information is being shared and consumed in the corporate workplace. If people can get addicted to social communications, why can they not get equally engaged with information that matters? What can we learn about information sharing from the consumer world that is relevant to enablement leaders? How can we apply lessons learned from the consumer world to better enable our teams?

The effects on companies, enablement leaders, and content creators are profound as we improve employee productivity and employee engagement.

In this chapter, we look at how modern trends like Facebook, Instagram, Snapchat, YouTube, and the proliferation of mobile apps are accelerating a corporate appetite for bite-sized, snackable content that can be consumed easily and quickly.

Make Content Attention Grabbing

There is a secret to getting your words heard, understood, and then reshared. Here are tips to help you make content attention grabbing, high impact, and action oriented. This advice applies to any kind of communication. These insights may provide a good lesson for employees wondering why their messages are not being understood or why they might not be getting the promotions they want.

Answer "What's in It for Me?"

Good communication starts with establishing a sense of value. Answer the question "What's in for me?" when creating content, which will help you discover the value of your content for your audience. For example, while it is important to set the tone in communications about expectations, explaining the "why" is a great way to motivate action.

Be Personable

Give your content a personality by broadcasting your face as you communicate. There is no reason to hide behind slides—your teams want to see your face. They want to know who the inventors are. Looking someone in the eye will make content more impactful.

Visual

Using images and color and fonts to make messages pop is a great way to capture attention. We learn a lot from the social worlds of Snapchat, Instagram, and Pinterest. People click on faces and images they like.

Share User Generated Content

Content created by users (employees, partners, and customers) creates authenticity and validation. User generated content will be consumed more and is proven to be more effective. Prioritizing this kind of content is important because it reduces the time to create it and test it and share it. It's proven, so once you have it, all you have to do is make it readily available.

In Context

It is important to distribute content and use it in context of a real workflow. Share short introductory videos and informational documents on the first few days after a new hire begins a job. With a salesperson, share tools and short and relevant sales aids right before a customer meeting.

Just-In-Time

Content and communications should be just-in-time. We should distribute information to our teams when they need it most. If I'm meeting a customer, send me a case study or customer story video that helps me better understand how to talk with the customer. If I'm working an early stage deal, as a salesperson should send me prospecting and pitch materials. We want to make sure our people are prepared and ready all the time.

Measurable

It is important to know how your content is doing in the employee attention economy. What content is being consumed? How many views and downloads does it have? What content is helping employees be more productive? You want the hard, quantitative metrics.

In sales, it is good to know which tools are being used and how effective they are in helping salespeople close business. Track views, downloads, and pipeline influence by asset. Share scorecards highlighting the return on all sales tools created.

Engaging

Make sure your content is engaging by getting feedback on the utility of the content. Have your employees, partners, and customers give feedback on the effectiveness of the content. Content can be scored, or feedback can be shared as comments or through other types of survey. Content effectiveness and engagement is automated today in a modern content-management system.

Mobile

Content should be optimized for mobile use, just as websites are. You want employee tools and resources to follow your people everywhere they go and on every professional device they use to get their jobs done.

The communication of ideas and content through play-books is ready for innovation. In the marketing world, mod-ern marketers have evolved their marketing strategies and tactics. We have websites. We use Instagram. We are on Facebook to build and connect with fans. We tell stories. We use videos. We use images to punctuate concepts and messages. We measure effectiveness. We create conversation with our audiences.

The same is now true for our employees. Employee engagement is important to get right. How we communicate is as important as what we communicate.

Team Huddles

Every week the team should come together to meet, share best practices, and align on priorities. We should be applying the same principles of content effectiveness reviewed in the previous section to our weekly team meetings. As enablement professionals, it's our job to lead and run weekly or monthly team calls. These are sometimes run in a radio show format with guest speakers. We can do a one-size-fits-all approach for our stakeholders, or we can create communication calls by role. They are important and the foundation of winning enablement strategies.

Team huddles are also executed by managers. Hopefully our managers have them weekly. We can help them do this. Managers in general do not make enough effort to communi-cate in an engaging way that answers the questions of "what's in it for me?" They often don't create a space for a conversation where communication is bidirectional. That's where we come in as enablement leaders.

As enablement professionals, it is our job to create content that is huddle ready for managers. This means that we want to create content that serves as a meeting in a box. We want to create a library of content that can be used by managers and consumed by their teams in their weekly meetings. It means creating videos and assets that are organized well and inspire conversation and curiosity. We do this by adding suggested discussion points and exercises like role plays.

After hosting a team call, be sure to include a follow-up recap email. The weekly or monthly recap email newsletters reinforce what's new and set the tone for focus and priority. Including a theme is a great way to drive additional alignment.

Besides regular calls and emails, you'll need to start thinking about your content library to help you scale and to help you deliver more value to your teams.

Sales Process Assets and Content

Taking a lesson from sales, let us look at a company's sales process and sales methodology as an example of how to shift our enablement thinking from the old way to a new way. The foundation of a sales methodology is the sales stages to follow and the sales process questions to answer at each stage of the sales process. Everything flows from the stages and process. A typical set of stages for a technology company selling business-to-business software is—

1. Qualification
2. Discovery

3. Demonstration

4. Mutual Plan

5. Proposal

The way most companies communicate and train on a sales process is to turn these steps into a slide deck that is large and dense with information. The materials are loaded into a library, and then teams are emailed a link.

The better way to do this is to break the sales process into small pieces of content in multiple digital formats rather than a process playbook. The content is created in multiple digital formats.

Step 1: Qualification Content

This piece covers the tools that are needed by sellers, including buyer profiles and qualification questions. You can also include a short company overview presentation and a sixty-second elevator pitch. The content should succinctly discuss how to gauge if a customer is ready to buy by asking them some qualification questions. The content should have a short list of questions and guide sellers to spend less time with prospects that aren't ready to buy or aren't in a position to buy.

Step 2: Discovery Content

The discovery content is foundational to executing a successful sales process. Information gathered in a discovery conversation is used to build a solution and proposal. It is also used to negotiate pricing. Short discovery tips and best practices could be top-performer stories or recordings of actual customer conversations. Why not have salespeople record the top questions they ask their buyers that are proven to help them learn more about their customer? It is great to create video vignettes of top-performing salespeople showing their peers how they conduct effective customer discovery conversations.

These tips and tools are important because they help improve sales productivity. New salespeople will ramp faster by closing deals faster. Struggling salespeople will get access to content they need by learning from their peers.

Step 3: Demonstration Content

In this piece of content, it is ideal to serve salespeople short demonstration scripts, solution overviews, and product demonstration flows to share with customers. We want to help our salespeople by giving them tools and assets they need without having to create it themselves. We want our salespeople to sell versus spending time building content. I also think it's a good idea to share video examples of demonstration flows completed by top performers. Learn from the best.

We want to have our salespeople use templates that are served up at the right time and then filled in based on information collected in the discovery. We want to help our sellers shorten sales cycles by focusing on the story versus figuring out the format to use.

Step 4: Mutual Plan

A big part of any customer buyer process is alignment with champions and economic buyers who are the buyers making decisions to spend money. We need to win over champions and economic buyers. We do this by selling value and helping champions and economic buyers see a path to success. That is the goal of a mutual plan. The best professionals document detailed mutual plans with clear action items and ownership for salespeople, champions, and economic buyers.

Since we're trying to help solve problems for our champions and economic buyers, we want to ensure we have co-ownership of mutual-plan actions. For this, sharing content templates and examples along with coaching videos is the way to make this part of the process more efficient. When we serve up mutual-plan templates with suggested actions and direction, we help our people spend more time selling and less time trying to figure out how to sell and close.

Step 5: Proposal

After a decision is made, it is time to get to a close with signed documents. Many steps and content types are useful at this stage. Negotiation tips and negotiation gives and gets are short, bite-sized content that are ideally served up just in time for a negotiation. Proposal templates and other closing materials should, ideally, also be served in small pieces of content.

What Should Be in the Sales Content Library?

We live in an era where people expect a dynamic library of content that is searchable and personalized with content recommendations. The old static file repository of materials is not how we should be thinking of a modern content library. Before we get into the best-practice list, we should follow some fundamental principles. The library must be well organized. It must be visual. It must be searchable. And as best as you can, make it be a one-stop shop so your people aren't going to too many places to find what they need to be successful.

Here are some of the "must have" content items to publish in your sales content library. You don't need all the items. Use what makes sense for your product and go-to-market. With the sales process in mind, here are some examples of how to create bite-sized content. You'll ideally want to partner with marketing to create all this content, so you don't have to create all this material on your own.

Buyer Personas: Document your buyer profiles, including their roles, attributes, the problems we can solve for them, compelling or trigger events, and how to communicate with them. We want to create content that will help our salespeople truly understand what's most important to our buyers.

Elevator Pitch: Create a short elevator pitch with coaching on value, customer proof points, engagement, and length. Make this content available in video and text. Include the talk track and script if necessary. Compose both short and longer versions. Including documentation on a one-liner tagline to voice mail, to a thirty-second elevator pitch, all the way up to a two-minute elevator pitch is super helpful to sales professionals.

Corporate Presentations: Create a first-call presentation with slides and speaking notes. Share slide examples created and used by top performers. Have video recorded versions, too.

Email Templates: Create a central place for your teams to find and share their best email templates by persona and by sales stage. These winning email communications are hugely beneficial, especially for new hires.

Sales Process: Document and share the sales process. Include all documentation that will help salespeople understand how to move through the process faster. This includes sales methodology documentation, qualification criteria, stages, forecasting, activities, value calculators, and success tips. Include supporting materials to help use the sales and customer relationship management systems like Salesforce.

Competitive Battle-Cards: Include videos and exercises on competitive overviews, strengths, weaknesses, handling competitive objections, and planting traps. Also include a competitive landscape and matrix of all the players compared against one another.

Deal-Win Stories: Keep your win stories in one central location for your teams to search by segment, industry, buyer, geography, and product.

Customer Stories and References: Centralize customer references and customer stories in one place to make it easy for everyone to find them and use them. Create a library of stories of your customers that are both written and videotaped. Like the deal-win stories, the customer stories should also be organized by segment, industry, buyer, geography, and product.

Frequently Asked Questions: Write down the most common questions your teams are being asked and provide the answers to them.

Industry Trends and Whitepapers: Make the files easily available and searchable. They are important to help salespeople understand the context of what's going on in the industry and what analysts think of their offerings and their competitive offerings.

Organize the content visually in folders so they are easy for your teams to find and consume. You want to make sure the content in the library is powered by a modern content-management system that will serve the right content at the right time and in context to your teams.

Playbooks

The next step with content is to turn the individual files into playbooks. There is a lot of debate about what is a playbook. For the purposes of understanding the Enablement Process Map, we'll refer to the playbook as a collection of files and actions that help drive key metrics that are tied back to the go-to-market priorities. We see playbooks being created for sales plays or campaign or specific competitors or industries or product pushes. The playbook is a collection of materials that include the basics, like industry trends, buyer profiles, elevator pitch, customer stories, sales process aides, FAQs, and competition, to name a few. The playbook is organized in a sequence that helps to keep teams aligned on what to do and when.

Executive Communications and Broadcasts

Leaders set the tone with their visionary and clear communication. When a top leader sends an email, it gets read. Top executives are busy, and sometimes the best way to get their involvement is to ghostwrite their communications for all strategic initiatives. Even if employees know the notes are ghostwritten, they know the notes are approved by the top leaders. Weekly or monthly employee broadcasts are a great way to drive momentum and rally teams to share updates. We did this at Salesforce for each of the sales and customer-facing roles. We branded the calls "Sharing Success." Many enablement leaders today host weekly or monthly team calls, executive broadcasts, podcasts, or radio shows as a big part of the communications strategy of a successful enablement program. One of the first things I would do when developing an enablement program is start hosting regular calls to create transparent and open communication.

Lessons from Leaders

Leaders can use the video communications to prepare and inspire their teams to get in the right mindset as they kick off the year. These videos are all about alignment and celebration.

For leaders, especially CEOs, before sending an email broadcast, consider sending a video message. Video is personal and emotive. Video-based communication builds relationships between leadership and employees at every level. People follow leaders who look them in the eye and speak from the heart. Video helps make this happen at scale.

The former president of DocuSign, Neil Hudspith, kicked off every year with a personalized video message to his staff, initiated by John Hsieh, the vice president of sales enablement. Neil and John asked everyone to share their successes from the previous year and ask goals for the new year. It's a motivational act by senior leaders.

The first time Neil did this video, product marketing brought a video team to his office, and they got Neil in his element, overlooking the San Francisco Bay. He was comfortable and excited. He graciously thanked everyone for their amazing contributions and then challenged them to imagine what they could do in the coming year. As a response to Neil's video message, employees recorded hundreds of videos, made thousands of comments, and viewed the videos tens of thousands of times. The communication started at the top and trickled down to the teams. The powerful questions and the answers created a rich library of stories and best practices.

The questions that stood out to me were "What is your proudest achievement from last year?" and "What are your aspirations for the coming year?" In his message, Neil shared his answers to the two questions, which centered around value and the customer. As a result, he was able to set the foundation for a company culture that emerged in the responding videos. The words "customer" and "value" showed up thousands of times in the employees' personal videos. That's how teams are aligned, knowledge is shared, and experiences are institutionalized at corporations like DocuSign.

The best videos are short and to the point. Have them be focused on a theme. CEO and leadership videos should have a clear purpose. They should be recorded from the leader's home or office or somewhere meaningful to them. Our leaders should not be reading from cue cards. Their messages should be purposeful and authentic.

With tens of thousands of videos recorded by sales teams over the past few months, I'm privileged to witness culture grow and evolve. Watching CEOs ask questions and inviting teams to respond in heartfelt, sincere sixty-second shorts is priceless. Corporate tone and values are set top-down; culture is nurtured bottom-up. Video bridges the two by creating community.

Tips for Asking a CEO to Record a Video

Getting a CEO to lead by example does not happen by accident. Once they see the value, they will be engaged and creative on their own. They are busy, and getting them to commit time and energy to this goal will require planning. Follow these steps:

1. Let them develop their own personalized message.
2. Write out notes and aids you know work for the leader.
3. Go to them to get the content.

Enablement Calendar

An enablement calendar is great to map out timing and schedule across an extended period of time. The calendar of enablement activities seems relatively easy to do, but given all the competing priorities, the reality is that it isn't easy. Getting alignment across teams around priorities and time commitments is hard. How much is the right amount of time to allocate to sales planning, learning, coaching, and deal/account reviews?

Here is a good benchmark you can use to create more buy-in to your calendar. The number is based on how many hours our teams should be spending on enablement. The number is communicated in a range of hours. Six hours per month is low and ten hours is a good number, but some will say it is high. Getting to this number should be based on the go-to-market priorities and be a direct extension of the learning and coaching goals. The number needs to be approved by the leadership team, then communicated with clear expectations to the individual team members and managers. With an approved and agreed-upon number, individuals and managers can plan their time and accelerate their success.

Crowdsourcing

Advanced communications include crowdsourcing and other feedback loops like advisory groups. Crowdsourcing best practices of content, stories, and playbook execution is something everyone talks about doing, but they never do right. Getting the actual assets and artifacts of a sales process is hard work. Folks are busy, and they never make it a priority to share.

Here is a list of a few content items to crowdsource from your top performers:

- Winning sales presentations
- Emails with high open rates
- Winning proposals

Advisory groups are a great way to create a structured forum for conversations and feedback from stakeholders and community members.

KEY TAKEAWAYS

Creating compelling and relevant communications is not an easy task. There is a reason why enablement lives in marketing and why sometimes product marketers make great enablement professionals. Communications is a big part of the success of our enablement strategies. If we don't communicate clearly and with a voice that is motivational, we'll lose our people from day one. Here are some of the rules of communications:

- Make content attention grabbing and answer the question, What's in it for me?

- Build communication cadence with calls and emails that align the team with top go-to-market priorities.

- Bring your leaders to reinforce key messages and emphasize what's important to do right now, and remember that they'll need coaching too.

- Create a dynamic library that gives your teams everything they need to be successful.

- Always be crowdsourcing best practices and top assets created by your people and proven to win.

Chapter 9

Customer Engagement

Boosting attainment and improving how our teams engage with customers is about skills, tools, and mindset. You can train your people to be the best they can be. I have learned a lot about how to elevate engagement between customer-facing employees and customers. The standards of customer engagement must be consistent, and expectations must be clear. We must adhere to it across the entire buyer's journey, starting with interest and extending all the way to close. Here are three principles that have proven to be successful for me: First, instill a curiosity mindset in every customer conversation where your teams are asking questions, building relationships, and solving real business problems for your customers. Second, have your people be great at knowing and telling stories to create credibility, urgency, and action. Third, share and expect excellence in execution at every step of the sales process. We'll share many examples in this chapter, like meeting checklists and handwritten thank you notes.

As enablement professionals, it is our job to ensure that our teams are following the execution flawlessly across all steps in the customer engagement, from prospecting and value selling to reference selling and proposal creation to negotiations, cross-selling, and upselling. By now we have created the training and development plans and executed learning and coaching. We have also created content and communicated clear expectations. Now it is time to ensure that our teams are putting into practice all our playbooks and best practices.

It's Showtime

Mark Siciliano, a friend and colleague of mine who is an experienced enablement professional, invited me to speak to his team at his annual sales kickoff event. The theme of the event was "It's Showtime," and it was intended to create a parallel between performers onstage and salespeople selling. Now is the time to ensure that our teams are putting into practice all our playbooks and best practices. It's showtime for our salespeople as they are getting on calls, having meetings, and presenting solutions to their customers. After all the learning and coaching, it's time to execute across all the steps in customer engagement. I drove down to Carmel Valley and prepared for a keynote talk with hundreds of his sales professionals. The energy in the room was high, and the salespeople were eager to learn and ready to execute. I remember asking a question of the audience, and their hands shot up high.

The coaching I received from Mark as we prepared for my keynote helped me understand that we needed to focus on the fundamentals of customer engagement. We decided that we needed to get the team doing more discovery and being more curious. We needed the folks in the room to be better storytellers. We needed to have everyone be religious about their daily execution from meeting planning to meeting follow-up. We realized that building relationships was an art that needed to be reintroduced to the room. And finally, we needed to raise awareness of the importance of practicing and rehearsing presentations before every customer meeting. I loved it. This was right up my alley. I ended up doing a talk similar to this one over and over during the 2018 sales kickoff season.

Curiosity and Value Selling

Being curious and asking questions is how to uncover business problems and sell value. The founder of Selling Through Curiosity™, Barry Rhein, who is also a dear friend, taught me the importance of always asking open-ended questions, layering and probing questions, example questions, and quantification at every step of the buyer's journey. How else do we know what value means to our buyers unless we uncover and document what is valuable to them?

We must understand our customer's current situation, problems, impacts, ideals, and benefits.[10] We are able to take the answers to these questions and formulate customized presentations, mutual plans, and relationship-building strategies. We apply curiosity to the decision-making process, evaluation process, budgets, business justification, time frame, executive sponsorship, buyers and influencers, competitive landscape, obstacles, and cross-sell/upsell. (See figure 9.1.)

As enablement leaders it is our duty to keep the art of asking questions front and center for our teams, including our

---

10 Barry Rhein founded Selling Through Curiosity™ in 1988. This section is based on the Selling Through Curiosity methodology exclusively available through SalesHood.

salespeople and our subject-matter experts. When we train our people, we must always remind them how important it is to master the discovery process in the spirit of getting to value. That is flawless customer engagement and execution. We must also train and coach our product managers and subject-matter experts to be the experts in asking open-ended, layering and probing, and example questions. We must all lead by example.

Open-Ended	Layered & Probing	Example	Quantification

Quantify Business Plan

1. Current Situation
2. Problems
3. Impacts
4. Ideals
5. Benefits

✓ Decision-Making Process
✓ Evaluation Process
✓ Budget
✓ Business Justification
✓ Time Frame

✓ Executive Sponsorship
✓ Buyers and Influencers
✓ Competitive Landscape
✓ Obstacles
✓ Cross-sell/Up-sell

Customized Presentations » Mutual Plans » Relationship Building Strategies

Figure 9.1: Selling Through Curiosity Methodology

Sales Call and Meeting Checklist

Our proven sales meeting checklist is a great way to improve sales excellence and results. There are many reasons why we're seeing our sales professionals in the industry not embrace excellence in their sales meeting preparation, execution, and follow-up. I realize many new salespeople haven't been coached on what makes a great meeting. We enablement leaders have not done a great job mapping out expectations to our new salespeople about what good looks like. We haven't provided a proven sales meeting checklist to our sales teams.

Here's a proven sales meeting checklist of pre-meeting, during meeting, and post-meeting best practices and tips to follow and live by every day:

1. Have clear meeting goals and expected outcomes documented and stated in email before and after meetings.

2. Put agendas that are agreed to by your customers in meeting calendar invites.

3. Meeting agendas should start with introductions and customers' priorities/challenges review. Meeting agendas should close with discussion and time for questions.

4. Research the company and recent announcements and know how their business is doing. Understand the context of their industry, too.

5. Research the people attending your meeting and identify shared interests and shared executive connections.

6. Connect with meeting attendees on LinkedIn before meeting. Some people believe this should be done after a meeting. My point of view is that it's an important touch point when a prospect accepts your request to connect. Make the connection, and use your connection's response and speed of response as a gauge of their awareness. If they connect fast, then it may mean they are excited to meet with you. If they don't connect quickly, it could mean it's not top of mind. Both are important to know. Don't forget to personalize the message.

7. Reconfirm agenda and meeting attendee participation. It's good to do this the day before the meeting is scheduled to happen.

8. Prepare a list of discovery and qualification questions to ask the prospect. The questions should preferably be open ended. Share the questions with your internal team to get alignment.

9. It's a requirement and best practice to brief executives attending the meeting with you beforehand. Share with your executives the context, current situation, and everything you learned during company, industry, and executive research. Your executives are busy. Help them help you. Be clear on what their role in the meeting is.

10. Introduce meeting attendees at meeting outset, and let everyone have a voice. Go around and have people share their role and what they hope to get out of the meeting.

11. Take thorough notes, capturing your customer's words.

12. Listen more and talk less.

13. Watch the clock to begin and end meetings as promised. Leave time for questions and discussion at the end.

14. Recap meeting outcomes and next steps before ending the call.

15. Send meeting follow-up notes with clear action items the same day of the meeting using your customer's words.

If you're a new salesperson, print out this list and check off each item for every sales call until they are part of your DNA. If you're a millennial, this list is nonnegotiable. If you're a seasoned salesperson, I hope you find these back-to-basics reminders useful. If you're a sales manager, share them with your team and coach your team to achieve excellence. If you're a sales enablement professional, integrate these best practices with your sales process and sales onboarding. If you're a customer, hold your sellers to the highest standard of excellence.

The Proven Way to Do Reference Selling

There is no question that leveraging references in our sales and pursuits helps our teams close deals faster. The way we set up reference calls for success will define what our customer engagement experience is like for our buyers. How we prepare our buyers and reference customers with briefs to maximize conversations and reference call outcomes will determine the effectiveness of pursuit. It is the difference between winning and losing.

Here is a list of best practices that are proven and used by the many experienced enterprise sales professionals:

1. **Develop a references strategy for your deal/account, and identify ideal references.** Do your discovery and know what is top of mind for your prospective buyer. Discovery is key. How would you know what references are most relevant without knowing what problems they want to solve?

2. **Match buyers and prospects correctly.** Match personality, function, experience, and level between prospective buyer and customer reference.

3. **Ask permission from the customer to use them as a reference.** It goes without saying, but it's risky to not

ask permission before sharing a logo and story with a prospective buyer. You never know what your customer is thinking. It's also good professional etiquette.

4. **Share the customer-success story with the buyer.** Follow a best-practice storytelling framework and make your story emotional, quantifiable, and personalized. Close your story with the question: How does this customer-success story compare to your desired business outcome?

5. **Write an introductory email connecting the reference customer and the prospective buyer.** Position the reference call as networking and best-practice sharing. It's a great way for two like professionals to get to know each other. Make it a win-win.

6. **Send a separate email to the reference customer, outlining what the buyer is looking to learn.** Help them help you. You get extra points if you brief the customer on a call.

7. **Send a separate briefing email to the prospective buyer.** Outline the reference customer's solution, ROI benefits, and journey. Include suggested questions for them to ask based on what you uncovered in discovery. We should always reinforce to the company that they should be judicious with the reference's time.

8. **Send thank you emails.** Both the prospective buyer and reference buyer deserve the courtesy of a thank you email after the reference calls happen. Handwritten thank you notes work well too. The personal touch is classy and highly differentiated.

9. **Confirm with your prospective buyer that they got what they needed.** It's important to make sure that the call

went as planned. Perhaps another reference call needs to be scheduled. It's always good to be curious and ask.

10. **Share the deal outcome.** Make sure to follow up with the reference customer to let them know if the prospect became a customer. References like to hear if their support helped.

Executive Presentations and Proposals

An important part of the customer engagement journey is how our teams prepare and present value to their buyers. Quoting Mark Siciliano, "It's showtime." These are the moments we cherish and aspire to when we sell. It is our job as enablement professionals and coaches to get our teams ready. There is much we can do beyond providing templates. Don't get me wrong, the execute presentation and proposal templates are must-haves. They are enablement table stakes. We are not limited to that work, though.

I remember back in 2006 getting called up onstage at Salesforce by Marc Benioff and being recognized for an amazing product launch of our Partner Relationship Management (PRM) system. I remember getting recognized not for the amazing technical innovation we accomplished with the product but for the way my team and I rolled up our sleeves and helped our teams. We helped them prospect. We showed them how to ask questions. We role-played with them. We coached them. We created presentations together. We even helped them fill in requests for proposals. That's what enablement is all about. Going that extra mile and partnering with salespeople and sales managers, arm in arm, in region, and in deals is what builds trust and credibility. The best enablement professionals execute enablement with this kind of passion and commitment.

It's important that our teams also appreciate the importance of practice and dry runs. Why wouldn't we want to win every deal? The greatest athletes and performers on the planet understand and appreciate the importance of practice and striving to be the best version of themselves. When you think of greatness, who do you think of? The Beatles, Serena Williams, and Wayne Gretzky? Build a process inside of your sales enablement and sales management cadence where teams are required to practice their executive presentations before standing and delivering to their customers.

In the book *Outliers*, author Malcolm Gladwell writes that it takes roughly ten thousand hours of practice to achieve mastery. For example, The Beatles did many thirty-set weeks in their early days with hundreds of performances each year. Serena Williams, known for achieving greatness in tennis, spends two hours practicing on the court every day and hours in the gym. Wayne Gretzky shared in his autobiography how he spent countless hours practicing every day in his backyard ice rink. He wrote: "The harder you work every day, the better you'll become." We should strive for the same excellence in all our customer engagement processes, including executive presentations and proposals.

After sitting through and reviewing thousands of executive presentations, here is a simple outline that you can customize to your sales process and go-to-market. Keep the presentations focused on customer business problems, value, and next steps. Please note that these slide recommendations are a guide, and feel free to edit and reorder to suit your needs. The main point is to have a template and iterate it based on win/loss data, making it readily available in your sales content library.

- Slide 1—Agenda or executive summary
- Slide 2—Current situation or SWOT (strengths, weaknesses, opportunities, threats)
- Slide 3—Problems we're solving
- Slide 4—Quantifiable impact of the problems
- Slide 5—Solution overview and vision
- Slide 6—Benefits of the solutions
- Slide 7—Customer references and proof points
- Slide 8—Business case and financial justification
- Slide 9—Project success plan
- Slide 10—Next steps

When your teams create their versions of the executive presentation, as much as they can they should be using their customers' words and examples.

Negotiations

Many sales skills training programs and many books are written on the topic of negotiations. The purpose of this section is to help your teams engage in negotiation conversations with winning strategies. The way to do it is to be clear on what they can and cannot negotiate with their customers. Having clarity and transparency on what they can "give" and what they should "get" is a big part of executing successful negotiations.

A great best practice is to create a library of gives and gets that are understood and available to your teams. Most companies do not take the time to share the list, and many do not spend the time training and coaching their people on executing a winning give/get strategy.

For example, with my children some gives may be dessert and playtime, and some gets may be eating breakfast and doing homework. In a business context, some gives may include pricing, discounts, payment terms, and length of contract, to name a few. Some gets may include customer testimonial videos and reference calls. The principles are the same. We want our teams to understand what's most important to us and our buyers and negotiate accordingly.

Here is an exercise you can run with your teams in a deal review session or team huddle:

1. Pick a deal.

2. Write out your give/get strategy.

3. Share your deal story with your team.

4. As a team, create a list of give/gets.

5. Document the list and add it to the sales content library.

One final piece of advice is to coach your teams to rely on the answers they collected during their customer discovery conversations to know what is most important to your customers. Curiosity gives your teams more power in negotiations.

Self-Sourcing Pipeline and Prospecting

During a recent meeting, the leadership team of a company was very focused on building new business sales pipelines.

More specifically, they were more interested in having their quota-carrying salespeople self-source their own new business pipeline. Doing this should be considered part of the role and responsibilities of every salesperson. Some companies hire sales development and lead qualification people to offload from the quota-carrying salespeople. "Always be prospecting" is how we should think about customer engagement and the enablement process. Self-sourcing pipeline is an important process, so expectations need to be clearly communicated and measured.

The way we helped this company create the right prospecting mindset and outcomes was to create a prospecting boot camp that the entire team was required to complete. The team was distributed around the globe, so we ran the prospecting boot camp as a virtual event. We needed to do this to ensure we were applying the same prospecting standards and expectations with everyone. We had the team do the following:

1. Complete a territory plan.
2. Practice their elevator pitch and voice mails.
3. Share the prospecting email used by the buying persona.
4. Share their prospect outreach steps and actions.
5. Share success stories.

By following these methods to standardize prospecting engagement, we quickly saw the activity shoot up and the corresponding amount of self-sourced pipeline increase too. Within thirty days, every quota-carrying salesperson had generated hundreds of thousands of highly qualified new business pipeline.

Engaging Prospects

As we help our teams write emails, leave voice mails, and develop our prospecting outreach strategies, let's revert back to simple English. Let's write emails like humans. Let's leave messages as though we're leaving messages to fellow humans. Let's engage prospects as though they're humans rather than records in a lead or contact database.

Put yourself in the shoes of the person receiving the email you're writing or the voice mail you're leaving. Ask yourself—

- How would you respond?
- How would the email or voice mail make you feel?
- What action and outcome do you expect?

Be mindful of every word, statement, and punctuation you write and say. Less is more. Speak in plain English.

Here are tips to write prospecting emails that project positive, action-oriented human energy:

- **Catchy Subject Lines:** I'll argue that the subject-line real estate of emails is the most important part of an email. We have exactly five seconds to hook our busy human recipients. Executives decide to reply, delete, or review emails later based on what's written or not written in the subject line. Be action oriented. Tie the words in the subject line to what's going on in the world of the person being emailed.

- **Warm Introductions:** Be human and use real words like "hello," "hi," and "how are you?" Be mindful of the context of the time of year, week, and day of the week. It's great to keep it real by saying things like "I hope you had a great weekend" and "How is your summer going?"

- **Insightful Stats/Questions:** Pick a statistic or a quote that is thought provoking and insightful. In a polite way, include it in the email to catch the attention of the buyer. We want the readers of our emails to pause and think for a few seconds and say to themselves, "Hmmm, I didn't know that" or "Wow, if we realized that benefit to our business, the results would be amazing."

- **Proof Points:** Share customer proof points that relate stories to industry, size of company, and business challenge. Inspire prospects to act through the power of storytelling. Tell customer stories that are relevant, emotional, and quantifiable.

- **Call to Action:** Be clear and direct. Make the call to action short and clear. I was told once that an effective call to action is between two to five words. Also, we should only have one call to action per email.

- **Simple Signature:** There is no need to include a long list of ways a prospect can contact us. I'd avoid including your email, title, office number, fax, mobile number, Twitter handle, LinkedIn profile link, and any other ways of contacting. Keep it simple with first and last names and a best number to use.

The Magic of Handwritten Thank You Cards

One of the best ways to differentiate yourself is to show gratitude with handwritten cards in sales (and life). Handwritten thank you cards are great sales tools to use. A handwritten thank you card is good karma and good business. It's amazing to me how many sales professionals don't practice the art of handwriting a thank you card to a prospect or customer. It's a lost skill, and I'd like to help bring it back to the center of how we engage with our customers and partners. I love writing thank you cards, and I do it all the time. I write them to people that make introductions to me or leaders who speak at my conferences. I also write them to customers after they sign a purchase order. People remember the thank you card, and they appreciate it very much.

When I speak at kickoffs and sales training events about best practices in sales execution, I always close with a discussion on gratitude and thank you cards. I ask the room, "How many people closed a deal in the past thirty, sixty, or ninety days?" A bunch of hands goes up. I get the room to applaud and high-five each other. The energy goes up, and folks are happy and feeling good about themselves. Then I ask, "How many people who closed a deal sent a handwritten thank you note to a customer who bought from them?" Hands drop, and the room quickly becomes quiet. There are usually only a couple hands remaining in the air. It's a good lesson and an eye-opening and humbling experience for everyone in the room.

Handwritten thank you cards work because they are personalized. In a world of automated email outreach and too much spam, the personalized handwritten thank you card goes a long way to help your people stand out from the crowd. I do not recommend the kind of "handwritten" cards that are sent via a simulated handwritten note. You know what those kind of cards look and feel like when you get one. They kind of look personalized, and they kind of look handwritten, but they aren't. Grab a pen. Grab a thank you card. Make it real.

Handwritten thank you cards work because they help

build relationships with people you admire and want to work with. You connect with people in a real and human way. When I send a handwritten thank you card, folks remember it and appreciate it. They also call or text or email to say thank you back. It's amazing when that happens.

Handwriting thank you cards takes discipline. It's easy to put it off. If you don't do it when you think about it, too much time will pass, and you'll feel funny sending one months later.

As enablement professionals, it's our job to coach our teams to prioritize gratitude and send our customers hand-written thank you cards. Make it easy and accessible. Order branded thank you cards for your teams, and celebrate the win stories.

Here are some examples of when your teams should be sending handwritten thank you cards to customers:

- A customer organizes a great meeting onsite.
- Champion makes an introduction to an executive.
- Customer signs an order.
- Customer refers a new prospect.
- Customer makes a reference call.

Always be grateful and send handwritten thank you notes consistently and often.

KEY TAKEAWAYS

Enablement doesn't stop with training and onboarding. As you can see from this chapter on customer engagement, it's our role to enable our teams every step of the way across the buyer's journey. Our teams need more than just coaching and content delivered just in time. They also need and appreciate best practices and skills to execute customer engagement resulting in better customer experiences and more value to our customers. Why not strive to win every deal?

- Remember to provide your teams with customer-facing tools and templates they need to be successful.

- Help your teams have the right mindset and behaviors to always be curious.

- Use storytelling and customer references to build relationships and credibility.

- Help your teams execute every meeting and customer flawlessly.

- Create value with customized executive presentations and proposals.

- Create a culture of self-sourcing pipeline.

- Show your teams the way to always be grateful and differentiate with handwritten thank you notes.

Chapter 10

Achievements

I was asked to present at a sales kickoff meeting to motivate and educate a group of sales professionals on the merits of having a mindset of sales excellence. I love doing these kinds of talks. I presented on topics that ranged from prospecting and territory planning to selling and closing and building relationships with handwritten thank you cards. It was a simple yet impactful message about back-to-basics in sales and customer relationship building. My aim was to help the room of sales professionals walk away energized and motivated to push themselves to do great things. It was a kickoff, and it was the time to make big commitments to hit big goals. Everyone was engaged and taking notes.

Amy Itaya, an experienced sales professional I worked with at Salesforce, was in the room. Unplanned, she shared her personal story about her sales achievements and one big achievement in particular. It turns out that she and I had worked together on a deal while we were at Salesforce. Working together and following the principles of great sales execution, she closed a mega deal. The significance of the story aside from the deal achievement and commission benefit is how she and her family celebrated the win. The big commission check ultimately changed the lives of her and her family. Her husband had started a new business and the check provided a financial cushion.

Amy choked up sharing her story, and I witnessed a deeper sense of accomplishment on her face. People are motivated by more than just money. They are motivated by life experiences. They are motivated by being able to gift people with rewards, awards, and recognition.

As an enablement professional, you need to be mindful of all types of achievements and motivational drivers. You need to build a culture and cadence of celebrating and sharing successes. Yes, money is important, and it's a big driver, but showcasing top performers and recognizing their results will have a long-lasting impact on feelings of achievement. When you discuss achievements, you should include compensation, certifications, recognition, and celebration in your thinking and programs.

Scale Knowledge and Share Success Stories

Institutional knowledge is created when teams consistently share why and how they are winning. Getting teams to share early successes and winning-deal stories more frequently and efficiently is a proven way to share best practices. It is also a great way to get the highest levels in the C-level executive suite to engage in public recognition and learning.

Jake Hofwegen, a close friend and now the senior vice president of Revenue Operations at Yext, a fast-paced hyper-growth technology company, needed a way to quickly get up to speed. We talked about ways for him and his new leader-ship team to understand how and why his teams were win-ning. They had an upcoming sales kickoff event and decided to ask every one of their sales and customer-facing employees to record their biggest deal win. They gave them questions to answer, too. It was a structured way to capture multiple deal-win stories at scale.

Hundreds of deal-win stories were recorded. Thousands of peer comments and virtual high fives were shared. I was able to join them at their kickoff event and witnessed a video montage of the best of the best videos. It created culture and set the tone of the year to come. Their theme was "Crush It," and their teams recorded videos telling their stories of how they crushed it.

Even more importantly, Jake and the senior-most leaders found the exercise incredible because they were able to get up to speed quickly on how deals are won at Yext. They also learned a lot about what was working and what needed to be improved in their sales motion. Jake then used the top videos for new hires to review in their onboarding.

The Yext experience shows that asking teams to share their win stories in a structured way will create rich content that builds culture, drives up teams' morale, and creates a richer onboarding experience for new hires.

Be Grateful with Video Stories

There are many ways to be grateful and celebrate achievements. Some people share thank you cards and give gifts. Giving a speech at an event is another way to celebrate achievement. These are all meaningful ways to recognize people for their great work. Here is a story of a team who wanted to recognize their leader, Paul Evans, for his exemplary leadership.

We brainstormed some innovative ways to quickly and efficiently capture authentic gratitude videos from a group of distributed team members. We came up with the idea to have everyone secretly record a short video, no more than ten seconds, thanking Paul for his leadership contributions. They kept the video messages secret until the company event, when they played a gratitude video montage. I was invited to attend the event, and I saw the finished product along with the smiles, hugs, and tears.

Folks at every level in the company turned in videos. Dean Stoecker, the CEO, recorded a twenty-five-second video sharing how Paul "is a great leader who makes everyone better professionals and better human beings." I know how much of an impact this kind of CEO communication has on employee satisfaction and retention. It's the ultimate culture builder.

The gratitude videos turned a thank you message into a deep and human form of gratitude and connection. The videos were sincere and delivered with smiles and warmth. Enabling a company to openly share these kinds of stories and content is not easy. The project made everyone vulnerable, which made the result even more special.

Creativity flourished organically. Some folks used costumes and family members as props in their videos. Others told jokes, played instruments, and sang songs. It was great to see how positive everyone felt about the future of the company. The videos indirectly showed the sentiment of the culture. If I were a new hire, I would feel as though the company was a great place to work. The authenticity of the videos underscored that point.

Normally what happens at this company is that this kind of rich content is shared in one-on-ones but not broadly. Now the videos and best practices are shared with everyone in the company and also used to build their library of best practices for organizational learning and new-hire onboarding.

Sales Club Events

Over the years, I ran and participated in many sales club trips to reward and recognize top performers for exceeding their goals. The emotional impact and employee loyalty generated from organizing a special club trip for sales top performers cannot be overemphasized. Folks tend to host sales club events in vacation destinations such as Mexico and Hawaii in North America and Thailand in Asia.

You should take an active role in making sure that there is a plan and budget for these life-changing and memorable perks. Sales clubs are common for large companies. We had a sales club every year at Salesforce and Oracle. It's a great tradition in the technology world.

I'm just closing out my first sales club at our startup SalesHood, which is a small company. You might be wondering how a small startup is able to afford a luxury like a sales club trip. With the flights, the rooms, and the food, the cost per person adds up, but the impact is high. We brought together the top performers for a few days of rest and bonding. I could see in their eyes that it was a great decision. I took them to a nice place, which was a true luxury. The team ate and drank together in a sunny location in Mexico. I remember the first team dinner was a special experience. We made a toast and shared gratitude person by person. Folks felt appreciated.

We spent five hours at dinner that night. No one wanted to retire to their rooms. They were having so much fun.

The benefit of a sales club event are huge. Your team will feel appreciated. They'll want to return the next year. I believe my team will exceed their achievement goals to secure their spot on the plane to Mexico.

Celebrate Top Performers with Win Stories

One of the big benefits of using video to capture authentic stories and real experiences is that rich content is developed. Rich content is generated from individuals who can apply knowledge to real-life experiences. Employee-generated content is what individuals want.

There are many ways to capture rich content:

- Ask your teams questions about how they do their jobs, and ask them to record their answers on video.

- Walk through a process and get teams to share what's working and what's not working at each step of the process.

- Get your teams to record their success stories.

- Get your teams to record a winning customer story.

- Get your teams to share a lesson learned after a project has been executed.

Benchmarking Top Performers

There's immense value in investing the time to benchmark top-performer activity and knowing what top performers are doing to achieve success. You want to look at every detail. Look at emails, presentations, and customer calls. Emails will show you how they are communicating with champions and economic buyers and how they write to drive action and collaboration. Presentations will show how they sell value and create executive-level business cases. Customer calls will show you how they conduct discovery and handle objections. Listen to the call or read transcripts. Read the emails or look at summary word cloud maps. The technology is there. The onus is on you to invest the time and do the research. The detail in the activity matters.

You can also learn a lot by having your top performers record their stories. Ask them to answer questions that are mapped to your sales process and sales playbook. Their stories are pure gold and pure inspiration. Their word choice is relevant. Their emphasis on how they do research and what they focus on in their sales pursuits are the details that people need to hear. The underlying premise is that people learn from their peers and, better yet, from the best of the best. These stories are great to be told at kickoff events and during monthly kickoff calls.

Another great place to look is the planning and preparation of top performers in the early days of their career. Look at their territory plans and account plans. Imagine having the documentation of territory and account plans as a guide to success for everyone to follow.

Recognition

The ultimate in recognition is being celebrated by a manager in front of peers. It's hard to share commission statements and income forms, but it's not hard to share stories. The stories of wins and successes are what people want to hear. If you can weave recognition into your enablement initiatives and events, the motivation to push teams to do more will be more impactful.

Compensation

Chris Cabrera, CEO of Xactly Corporation and author of the book *Game the Plan*, spoke at the SalesHood customer conference about ways to tie together compensation and enablement to drive up attainment and achievements.

In his talk, he shared a lot about ways to measure and reward salespeople and sales managers to create win-wins and make the most money. Compensation is mostly viewed tactically instead of strategically and "is up to nine to ten percent of a company's revenue," according to Chris. Getting salespeople to do more is directly related to how well a compensation is designed. Dangling "sales incentive carrots" will drive behavior. The measures between the compensation plan and the go-to-market priorities drive behavior and outcomes.

Compensation plans need the right measures, timely communications, and transparency. Look at your business drivers and key performance indicators and set up compensation incentives that are tied to exceeding revenue and activity goals. If you want to drive up revenue in a certain product, then include a compensation trigger that incents your people to focus on that product. The expression "do you want fries with your burger?" is a great way to think about motivating your sellers to sell add-on and upsell products. Chris says that three compensation plan measures are ideal. "The data across hundreds of thousands of people across the globe covering billions of transactions proves that plans that have one measure are good, two are better, and three are best."

Communications is all about telling your teams what they will be getting in a clear way and in a timely fashion. Getting the compensation plan out weeks and months after a year, month, or quarterly kickoff is not good practice. The compensation plan should be a carrot that is used to achieve more. Transparency is about sharing results and achievements openly. It is also about sharing achievements in a form that is better than a spreadsheet. I believe we should make our plans easy to understand and appealing to review. Achievements should be celebrated, and it starts with the compensation plan.

The data that Chris is referring to is factual because it is based on paying salespeople. It's richer than sales data from a sales system like Salesforce or Microsoft Dynamics because it feeds accounts payable. People get paid based on the measures in their compensation plan. It is fact grounded in money. The art of getting compensation right is to ensure that the values are optimized to drive the right behaviors.

Team Toasts

The words spoken to celebrate achievements matter. It's important to celebrate success and recognize where you came from and how much you accomplished. It's good to reflect on all the hard work it took to get to the achievement milestone you're celebrating. Always recognize and celebrate the people who made magic happen. In the gratitude, share some words about each person. Highlight why each one is significant and how they impacted the business. Help your managers and leaders by coaching them on their notes and toasts. Have them go person by person or group by group in as much detail as time permits. Then, have them look to the future and motivate people to aspire to do more. Challenge everyone to reserve their spots by achieving greatness again. The formula for the toast can be applied to a speech or can be a framework for an email. The toast is a metaphor for communicating gratitude for small achievements and big achievements. It all matters.

KEY TAKEAWAYS

It's time to celebrate and recognize your team's achievements. Here are a few ways to express gratitude:

- Give the gift of experience by hosting a top performer special club trip somewhere really nice.
- Give the top performer a special gift like a watch or something they'll always remember.
- Schedule private, one-on-one time with your top performers and your CEO.
- Celebrate (and toast) the best by recognizing top performers at a dinner and/or during sales kickoff keynotes.
- Have your top performers record win stories to celebrate successes with storytelling. (When the ask comes from senior leadership, it's extra special.)
- Send out video win stories celebrating the best of the best, creating waves of virtual high fives.
- Celebrate top performers and document what they do to win.

- In addition to the commission checks—which are very important—give out trophies and award certificates for high achievers, biggest deals, and rookie of the year.
- Ask people to share videos and notes highlighting peer gratitude.
- Say thank you for a job well done.

PART THREE

PRIORITIES

Chapter 11

Manager Enablement

The strength of a company is defined by the competency of its managers, the ones who lead a team of individual contributors. However, most managers have never been trained to develop their teams. This is a big problem. What we do not talk about enough is the importance of investing time to develop managers to help them learn to develop their people. We assume they are doing this. Rather than expecting our managers to pick up the slack and do the work of their teams, they need to be amazing at asking open-ended questions about activity, data, and process to change their mindsets, behaviors, and outcomes.

An effective manager creates a space to have a collaborative coaching conversation by giving their people the responsibility of ownership and accountability across every facet of their jobs. In contrast, ineffective coaching and talent management happens by micromanaging people, asking them closed-ended questions, not creating a space for a coaching conversation, and not holding them accountable to follow the process.

The goal of this chapter is to highlight the importance of prioritizing coaching and enabling your front-line managers.

This is something that is talked about a lot but never fully executed. Other priorities always take precedence.

The ROI of Sales Coaching

Getting sales teams to be more productive and close more business faster is a top priority for many companies. The sales productivity conversation is making its way to the executive boardroom. There is general belief that better sales coaching will result in more revenue. Sales force enablement grew from 19.3 percent in 2013 to 32.7 percent in 2016. Quota attainment decreased from 63 percent in 2012 to 55.8 percent in 2016 from data reported by CSO Insights.

According to Tamara Schenk, sales enablement leader and analyst research director at CSO Insights, "Sales coaching is a leadership skill that develops each salesperson's full potential. Sales managers use their domain expertise, along with social, communication, and questioning skills to facilitate conversations with their team members that allow them to discover areas for improvement and possibilities to break through to new levels of success."[11]

It is amazing how many sales professionals are not hitting their revenue goals. According to the *SaaS Incentive Compensation Benchmark Report*, 79 percent of sales representatives miss quota, and 14 percent never achieve even 10 percent of quota. Across the entire SaaS data set, the average

---

11 Tamara Schenk, "Sales Coaching: How to Get It Right," tamaraschenk.com, Sept. 7, 2017, http://blog.tamaraschenk.com/sales-coaching-how-to-get-it-right/.

quota attainment is 58 percent. The data remained consistent regardless of tenure.[12]

Barry Rhein, founder of Selling Through Curiosity™ and Coaching Through Curiosity™, poses a thoughtful question: "What are the ways we can tweak our thinking and skills to create greatness in our people?"

Why aren't companies doing more sales coaching? What are companies doing to help increase the number of salespeople who hit quota? How are we enabling our managers to be better coached?

Barry Rhein is a big proponent of helping mangers apply curiosity to developing their teams. Barry has a profound metaphorical piece of advice: "Do you give your team a fish or teach them to fish?" What if managers could develop their teams so they can be stand-alone, closing business on their own? Great managers are able to develop their teams to setup their own deals to win. Great managers ask the right questions to help their teams fix and close their own deals.

Why Is Coaching Hard for Managers?

Many front-line managers struggle with coaching and developing their teams although they are past top performers. Among the reasons are—

- They are not trained to coach and develop their teams.
- They lack the skills.
- They do not know how to give constructive feedback.
- They do not ask developing questions.

---

12   SaaS Industry Incentive Compensation Benchmark Report published by Xactly Corporation in 2013.

- They do not believe they have the time to do effective coaching.
- They do not prioritize real coaching.
- They spend too much time working deals instead of coaching reps on executing the right behaviors on deals.

Great managers invest time to review their team's work. Great managers share real-time constructive feedback. Great managers use one-on-ones, deal reviews, and team huddles to accelerate coaching moments on industry knowledge, product mastery, sales execution, storytelling, and communication.

Inspired by Barry Rhein, here are some curiosity-based coaching techniques for managers to ask reps different types of open-ended questions.

OPEN-ENDED DEVELOPING QUESTIONS WORK WELL FOR DEAL COACHING:

- What questions are you planning to ask your customer?
- What did the customer actually say?
- That sounds like an assumption. How do we find out what the customer said?
- How will you prioritize what needs to be done?
- What do we do next?
- What concerns do you have about accomplishing your goals?
- How are you going to get this deal back on track?
- What can you do to make this a perfect deal?

- What are your action items based on what we talked about today?
- What else can you tell me about . . . ?
- What do you mean by . . . ?
- How did you come up with . . . ?
- How so?
- Why is that?
- What are your thoughts on . . . ?
- What are some more examples . . . ?
- How would you measure . . . ?

Successful managers give feedback to their teams in one-on-ones and team huddles daily, weekly, and monthly, not just at performance reviews or when results are not going so great.

Sales Manager Enablement Case Study

Bruce Campbell from Sage Intacct is an amazing sales enablement professional who delivers results while keeping his enablement fun and engaging with skits, music, and game shows. He is leading the charge with manager coaching. In an interview we did together, Bruce shared: "It would be irresponsible to not include some sort of sales management enablement inside a general sales readiness foundation and scope."[13]

---

13   Go to the ten-minute mark of the video to hear Bruce discuss Sales Manager Enablement, "SalesHood Live! Bruce Campbell – Director of Sales Enablement at Sage Intacct," YouTube, Mar. 9, 2018, https://youtu.be/ JplMNNWFg3U.

Bruce started his sales manager enablement journey by including some third-party manager training in the area of coaching to help managers understand the difference between coaching and normal interactions with staff, as well as learning about the different kinds of coaching that exist. They took advantage of having all managers together during their annual sales kickoff and gave them this training in person. They were focused on building a coaching culture.

What's unique about the work Bruce is doing with his managers is that he and his senior leaders have set coaching goals for their managers. "Every manager all the way up to the senior vice president level has to have at least two coaching sessions a month with their employees." The results of this sales manager enablement initiative are positive. They track all the coaching sessions and activities, allowing for full visibility up the chain of command but keeping the coaching conversations and feedback confidential to that specific chain.

Managers have a coaching quota, and they are required to document their coaching conversations. The documented coaching conversations are then sent to their managers. Here are the questions the managers answer after every coaching conversation with their employees:

- What was the date of your coaching session?
- Who did you coach? Please input first and last name.
- What was the coaching situation?
- Which of the five coaching "hats" did you use?
- What was the outcome of your coaching session?

Managers are coaching managers on how they coach their employees. Since the managers are documenting their coaching conversations, their managers get notified and play active roles in sales manager enablement.

Senor leadership is noticing huge improvements in managers' quality of coaching given by the sales managers and are enthusiastic about how this coaching culture is impacting field sales relationships and the maturity of the management staff.

Good Coaching versus Bad Coaching

Matt Cameron is an experienced sales leader who leads an organization that enables and certifies managers on sales management best practices and skills. He says: "Every manager needs management training on how to coach and develop their teams. The tell-tale sign that manager coaching is needed is unpredictable revenue results and managers can't defend their forecast, that's a clear sign that there's a problem." Other indicators that managers need training include hiring goals not being met, team attrition, and variability in attainment with the team and you don't know why. Matt went on to share what bad coaching looks and feels like: "Bad coaching feels like scary interactions with my unpredictable boss, and I don't know what the outcome is going to be, resulting in employees walking into every meeting ready to defend, duck, and dive. Employees then close up and don't share, which means you can't coach properly."

Then I asked Matt what good coaching looks and feels like. He answered: "Employees feel like sitting down with a manager is going to be a growth opportunity. Every time they have a coaching session, employees learn something new and they are better for it and they develop, and at the end of it the relationships are strengthened."

In Matt's program he trains and certifies front-line managers in sales process and methodology, forecasting, high-performance coaching, sales culture, inspection and operations rigor, recruiting, sales enablement, feedback and difficult conversations, managing up, deal structures, and contract terms. The program is remarkable.[14]

I really like the discussion and guidance Matt provides on the five roles managers must play and why. Here are the five roles:

Coach: A manager coach is ultimately responsible for the performance, production, and engagement of reps. Use this role when you feel the rep needs to come up with ideas and fixes to get to the root of their issues and resolve them themselves.

Leader: A manager leader sets and defines the organizational and/or team vision. Use this role when you have an issue that impacts the team or alignment to the team's culture, chain of command, or mission statement.

Manager: A manager practices and implements policies and procedures that mitigate risk, and drives productivity to ensure goals are met. Use this role when pure productivity is the main issue and performance failure is the topic to handle.

Mentor: A manager mentor is someone who can advise based on their own personal and professional experience and expertise. Use this role when asked for advice or experiential opinions or when stories from your past can make a point.

Trainer: A manager trainer is someone who really knows the staff's job but just can't do it all themselves. Use this role

---

14 You can learn more from Matt from this interview conducted on December 1, 2017: "SalesHood Live! Matt Cameron – Managing Partner at Sales Op Central," YouTube, Dec. 1, 2017, https://youtu.be/TaRt-sHY34M.

when training is required and you know exactly what they need and can own their improvement by your hand or by someone else's.

Evaluating Your Coaching Activities

This section will help you evaluate the frequency, quality, and impact of coaching activity performed by you and your managers. It's a great guide to share with your front-line managers, too. Ask your managers how they are doing against these coaching best practices:

Make Every Moment a Coaching Moment

Give feedback frequently. Be consistent. Do not wait. Use team meetings and one-on-ones to share feedback as it is happening.

Make Sales Coaching a Team Activity

The best managers are consistently, frequently, and openly giving the team feedback. Turn coaching into a regular activity like pipeline reviews.

Explain the "Why"

Communication is critical to changing behavior. The best sales managers are clear about expectations and value. They always kick off meetings and initiatives explaining the "what's in it for me" to the team.

Start Positive and Always Be Encouraging

Begin a review or feedback session on a positive note. Highlight strengths and growth over time. Even constructive feedback should be positive.

Empathize and Appreciate

Recognize how hard your team is working, and share accolades like "I know how hard it is to get our deals across the finish line." Put yourself in their place when giving feedback. Lead by example. When a developmental growth area is identified, use phrasing like "Let's see how we can work together."

Share Specific Examples

Giving feedback and coaching in generalities does not help reps and teams develop their skills and improve their work. For example, if a rep is behind on pipeline development, be specific about how much pipeline should be developed and how to develop it.

Tell the Truth, Even When Inconvenient

Speak clearly and specifically. Make sure your team knows where they stand.

Help Open Mentorship Relationships

When coaching and giving feedback, share best-practice examples from others. Be a connector within your team and in your broader work community to facilitate mentorships. For example, if your team is doing a pitch practice, highlight other pitches that would be good for folks to watch to improve their own.

Suggest Areas of Growth

It is our job to get our teams to be their best. Even when someone is doing great, they always have areas where they can grow. Push people to think about ways to grow personally and professionally and to shoot for even higher goal achievement.

Be Human

Be sure to thank teams for their hard work, and verbally appreciate extra effort, too. Use humor to put challenges into perspective. It is a best practice to smile and keep ongoing coaching feedback a bit light and fun.

Creating knowledge and reinforcing the practice is a skill that front-line managers need to have, but most haven't been trained, and many lack the tools and resources to be successful. Being prescriptive with managers of their role in territory planning, quarterly business reviews, deal reviews, and onboarding is a great step to help managers create a coaching culture.

The Role of Managers in Onboarding

An important step that is often overlooked is including front-line managers in the onboarding process of their new hires. It starts by sending your managers reports and updates on the progress of their team members. They'll appreciate it. Encourage and expect your managers to review the pitches and presentations when they've completed onboarding their new hires. Have your managers share notes of support and encouragement along the way. Ghostwrite them if that helps ensure they get it done. Hold your managers accountable for coaching and supporting their own team members during their onboarding path.

Managers will see huge benefits if they follow the onboarding best practices described below.

Give Context

Managers are the perfect ones to give their new hire context. Managers should simultaneously be taking their teams through the onboarding journey alongside the coaches and enablement professionals. They will accelerate results and drive up productivity by sharing their lessons during their own personal onboarding. They are the most qualified to emphasize key topics, as they know what works, and they also know the personality and skills of the new hire.

Prioritize and Focus

Managers are great at providing additional prioritization so the new hire isn't overwhelmed. When the new hire starts consuming content and meeting people, everyone gives what seems like great advice. A manager will help their new hires remember what is most important to their success path and remind them why they were hired, over and over again. Confidence building is critical in this learning phase. That's the role of the manager.

Schedule Daily One-on-Ones

Managers with experience hiring and retaining new hires will also proactively schedule time with their new hires. The human touch is critical here, especially for building trust and a relationship with a new manager. A daily check-in by phone or in person is a great best practice. Suggest to your managers that they schedule a fifteen-minute call every day for the new hire's first four weeks on the job. A new hire will then have the advantage of seeing how much their manager cares about their success. And a manager gets the chance to be at the pulse of what their new team member is doing and thinking.

Find Early Wins

Another tip that you can share is to remind the manager how important early wins are. Have the manager plan a project, assignment, or task that becomes an early win. The manager should help the new hire build their confidence and put these early points on the board. Once the job is successfully completed, the manager should celebrate the win broadly. The more the merrier when it comes to early wins and celebrating successes.

Managers are busy running their business and helping their team be successful. Bringing on a new hire takes time. Remind them of their role in the success of their new hires.

KEY TAKEAWAYS

Don't forget that your front-line managers need enablement too. You will get a lot of enablement leverage and scale if you put the right amount of focus on enabling your front-line managers. Make it a part of your enablement charter from day one to avoid falling behind. There is tremendous return on investment in enabling your managers to do better coaching. Here are four final tips to remember as you focus on manager enablement as a top priority:

- Coaching is hard and does not come natural for front-line managers. Remember, most were top performers who never received any kind of management coaching.

- Provide your managers with coaching guides and playbooks.

- Hold your managers accountable for coaching and developing their teams.
- Help your managers understand the difference between good coaching and bad coaching.

Chapter 12

Kickoff Events

Jake Hofwegen, SVP revenue operations and strategy at Yext, decided that he and his team wanted to crowdsource win stories across their revenue teams. They wanted to engage their teams in active learning before the teams attended their annual sales kickoff event. Normally, win stories are shared in keynotes at events. They challenged every sales professional, channel team, and customer-facing employee at Yext to record a short video deal-win story. Their teams recorded more than 260 win stories, and their win stories were peer reviewed and watched more than two thousand times. They even showed some of the biggest and most creative deal wins at their kickoff event. The accelerated revenue outcomes were the result of sharing stories broadly and the act of recording and peer reviewing stories to help their teams learn the sales best practices faster.

At DocuSign, John Hsieh, vice president of sales enablement, and Jeff Leslie, director of field communications, engaged their teams in new ways at their sales kickoff event. Their sales kickoff event and year theme was "Achieve." They asked their teams to answer two questions with a video story answer:

What was your biggest achievement last year, and what are you aspiring to achieve in the coming year for yourself, your customers, and DocuSign?

Hundreds of video stories were shared along with thousands of peer reviews and views. The outcome here is a fast start to exceeding their goals. Their teams recorded motivational stories. Engagement was high. Goals were set publicly. The virtual high-fiving of learning and sharing goals was a great way to get their teams aligned and doing the best work possible. Like Jake at Yext, they showed the best videos. What a great example of active learning and active participation by employees at a company kickoff event.

Aaron Farley, when he was global head of enablement at Apttus, and his leadership team were committed to building a culture of learning with prework before every sales kickoff. They, too, believed in embracing active learning principles. They believed in getting started before the event with five hours of prework, including product training, new pitch deck reviews, sales process best practices, and competitive updates. Apttus boasts more than 90 percent completion of their sales kickoff prework year after year. Their teams do the prework, and they appreciate learning the enablement team's thoughtful, well-curated content. By creating short videos and knowledge checks to be completed before the event, the enablement team promotes more active learning and participation at their event instead of boring everyone to death with PowerPoint presentations.

These leaders and examples should motivate and inspire you to creatively come up with ways to increase engagement and active learning. These are great examples that all resulted in high engagement and accelerated learning outcomes. The examples were executed by enablement leaders who are strong practitioners who exemplify enablement mastery. The goal of this chapter is to provide clear direction on how to execute kickoff events in a fun, engaging way with proven results.

The New Sales Kickoff

Much is written about what to do and what not to do at sales kickoffs. I want to get really tactical in order to get strategic about outcomes. One of the best sales kickoff events I had the good fortune to help organize was in 2016 with one of our customers at SalesHood, Blair Crump, who was the chief operating officer at the time. As much as I appreciate all the great events we ran during my time at Salesforce, this event we planned and executed together was something truly special. With a few short weeks before the event, we decided to plan and execute the most engaging kickoff event ever with active learning before, during, and after the event. We started working together mid-December for an early January sales kickoff event. Time was critical. Every day mattered. We did not want to lose a quarter, and we wanted to hit the attainment numbers for the quarter and get a fast start on the year.

Kickoff Goals and Plan

The first step in our journey was to diagnose the issues and build a sales kickoff plan that was aligned with our sales enablement and revenue goals. We concluded that the company had issues with messaging, sales execution, and sales discipline—issues across the sales strategy board. The corporate pitch was not consistent. Compelling events were not uncovered in deals, and mutual plans were not completed either. Deals were also not updated in their sales system. Their teams were not saying the right things to customers. They were not executing the right sales playbook consistently. They were not reporting back to their managers what was going on in their deals. We had a lot of work to do. With this information in hand, we created an amazing program that moved the needle in weeks instead of months. Our goal was to accelerate learning by front-ending the event with assessments, surveys, and pitch practice to better inform our event agenda, keynotes, and workshops.

Kickoff Prework

We identified content and learning goals that we carried through the prework, onsite event workshops and post-event reinforcement.

We filled the prework with content and coaching around the sales execution and messaging topics needing improvement. The CMO, Patrick Schneidau, created videos on the corporate pitch along with speaker notes and coaching aids. Participating teams were required to watch the videos and record their own pitch. Then they were asked to review and score at least three peer pitches. Patrick quickly knew where improvements needed to be made simply by listening to a few pitches. The prework path was enriched with sales process videos on topics like compelling events and mutual plans mapping to the goal of improving sales execution. The teams watched the videos, and then they were asked to pick a deal and share the compelling event for a deal and draft a mutual plan. They did all this asynchronously before the event. Every salesperson was asked to complete the sales execution tasks, and managers reviewed and provided feedback too. Finally, each person was asked to answer questions about their goals for the upcoming year and their obstacles to achieve them. The answers to these questions were highlighted in one of the event keynotes.

Everyone showed up to the event ready and pumped up because they had started collaborating and engaging with their peers ahead of time on topics aligned with revenue and company goals.

Normally what happens at sales kickoff events is that an equivalent amount of content is shared at the event and not delivered as prework. By introducing the content before an event, the learning started early (before the event), and the path to successful outcomes was accelerated. With this approach, answers to the questions are reviewed before the event and used in keynotes and workshops. Everyone learns, including the leadership team. By following this approach and best practice, senior leadership accesses the sentiment and knowledge of their teams much earlier. They are able to use this information to shape their keynotes and interaction with teams at the event.

What we did next was truly game-changing.

The entire event agenda mapped to the prework content. The sessions at the event were a direct follow-up from the online prework. The answers to the questions and pitch recordings became content used in the workshop to accelerate learnings and business outcomes. The speakers aggregated answers and were coached to incorporate observations into their presentations. The pitch videos from the top performers were shared onstage. Besides celebrating the best practices, the leaders was able to share real insights into where the teams did well on the pitches and where their pitches could be improved. Normally this cycle of reinforcement would span six to twelve months instead of days and weeks.

The sales leaders could uncover sales execution issues

around compelling events and mutual plans now instead of at the end of the quarter. Rather than seeing issues bubble up from missed deals and bad forecasting, the teams were educated on ways to overcome challenges they were going to face. The sales leaders could easily diagnose what was happening and what needed to be improved in real time because the sellers diligently completed the prework. Their prework submissions were as material as real-deal activity. Their observations were addressed in workshops during the sales kickoff agenda. The managers showed word clouds of their team's answers and highlighted where the teams were slightly off in their thinking. They started their workshops with those insights, captured the attention of their teams by using the team's words, and drove down sales-cycle time. They accelerated outcomes and sales coaching from years and months to weeks and days.

After the event, to get certified the teams were asked to redo their pitches and complete their exercises again with the feedback and coaching in mind. The results were spectacular. The teams systematically went through and completed all of their certifications and deal coaching.

The organization had a great quarter and built a strong foundation to overachieve and improve all their sales metrics. Engagement was super high. I spoke to many of the team members, and they overwhelmingly said it was the best sales kickoff they had ever experienced because of the orchestration of the content before, during, and after the event.

The Best Agenda for Sales Kickoffs

Sales kickoffs serve a dual purpose: to celebrate the past year of success and to set the tone and goals for the new year. It's important to create a kickoff and agenda that's the right mix of celebration, motivation, conversation, action, and storytelling.

It's all about human connection and making people feel as if they're part of something much bigger. Your perfect agenda needs to give attendees the context of why and also bring them together—whether in person or at a virtual kickoff. If you aren't working this into your agenda now, it's time to get started. Here are just a few ways you can make a huge difference in the effectiveness of your sales kickoff agenda this year and for years to come.

Share "bigger than you" motivation. Of course, a successful sales kickoff instills the motivation to keep sales reps and leaders going all year long. But that motivation needs some back-up support in the form of inspiration and clear, transparent, and open communication of goals, expectations, and metrics. A sales team can only be the best they can be if they know what success should look like—and if you make it personal to them.

The agenda should include a clear articulation of not only goals from the most senior leaders but also the "bigger than you" motivation. Think about Elon Musk at a launch or kickoff. It's not just the electric car; it's the entire message that team members are there to change the world and make it a cleaner, healthier place. Communicating the difference your company makes to the lives of your customers—or the world at large—will deliver the motivation that everyone is part of something much larger. And, of course, be specific and prescriptive with what your team should do to help make that vision a reality. Present the big picture, then clarify each person's role in the big picture.

Create Breathing Room

With a one- or two-day agenda, there is the motivational piece and then there's the drilldown into the tactics. What will a sales rep's life look like over the next thirty, sixty, or ninety days? Communicating specifics is crucial. But be sure to leave time in the agenda for people to actually talk about the details.

This is another moment where you can bring the element of human connection into your agenda. If you inspire people with amazing energy and motivation but don't allow them to breathe and converse, then you have missed the real synergy that can happen to bring the goals to life after the kickoff.

These conversations can take the form of engaging workshop exercises to discuss the motivational topics and goals at an in-depth and personal level. Drive a discussion of "what it means to me and my role." And don't lose the valuable content produced there. Workshop leaders should collect the sentiments; the final session of the agenda could include a summation of the thoughts and "what we've been hearing from you." The motivation comes full circle because teams are now directly involved and active participants.

Encourage Peer Networking

New connections can also be created with peer networking. Help people meet each other who wouldn't normally meet—whether due to different territories, departments, you name it. You can do something tactical and informal during the introduction of a session by saying, "Everybody walk up to somebody you don't know and tell them your biggest accomplishment from 2017." And you truly get the energy going in the room. It works with ten people, fifty people, or a thousand. If you're doing a virtual kickoff, you can also make this work with video conferencing and chats to help break down that digital barrier.

You can also take a more formal approach to facilitate these interactions and conversations. Why not let developers meet salespeople? Why not let customer support people meet developers? Why not let salespeople meet marketing people? Get people to share and talk with others they might not ever connect with, and introduce their ideas to each other.

True inspiration and innovation can happen when we break out of our own bubbles. In the end, it's all about driving human connection through conversation—and the best discussions are those around the themes and motivations anchoring the overall kickoff and the ultimate drivers of business success.

Now, let's explore a checklist you can share with your teams to get everyone aligned on what works and what doesn't work so well with kickoff events.

The Definitive Kickoff Checklist

Over the years, we have participated and led hundreds of sales kickoff events. We know what works, and we know what doesn't work so well. I reflected on my deep experience to create a list of sales kickoff planning and execution tips. I shared the list on LinkedIn and crowdsourced the definitive Sales Kickoff Checklist from leaders around the world who contributed their experiences. Interest in this topic is high, so we created a sales kickoff checklist:

1. Avoid having people sit for more than thirty minutes without music or video stimulation.

2. Create a strategy that involves prework to do before events.

3. Give reinforcement learning after the event to keep momentum going.

4. Document a vision for content publishers and event participants to understand.

5. Align with company culture.

6. Include all quota- and non-quota-carrying employees in an event that flies people to a central location.

7. Celebrate customer stories, deal wins, and top performers.

8. Include top performers onstage to share their successes.

9. Include healthy snacks and coffee throughout the event.

10. Do more inspiration, alignment, and motivation instead of too much product training.

11. Avoid rolling out new, untested technology that leaves people with more frustration than benefit.

12. Avoid running keynotes as death by PowerPoint presentations without active attendee engagement.

13. Schedule time to rehearse presenters and practice presentations before showtime.

14. Avoid sharing department updates onstage at the event. Save the updates for follow-up notes, emails, or video calls.

15. Don't try to do too many things at once.

16. Do a lot of networking and peer collaboration.

17. Keep expenses down by booking hotels and flights early.

18. Measure the impact.

19. Don't work hard and play hard. You can't do both.

20. Make room for downtime.

KEY TAKEAWAYS

Kickoff events are an important part of company alignment. They energize and align teams by bringing people together in person or virtually. They are intended to be motivational and to support activities only possible to do together as a group. They are not intended to be a year's worth of training in one week or a few days. Be careful of trying to do too much in a single kickoff event.

Work with your leaders to create agendas that are mapped to your go-to-market goals and company priorities. Follow the tips and best practices in this chapter, and refer to the kickoff checklist before every event. Circulate it to planning teams to get everyone aligned with these proven best practices. Make your kickoffs great by putting yourself in the shoes of your teams, and don't forget the basic principles of human engagement and knowledge retention.

Chapter 13

Modern Corporate University

I remember getting on a call with a chief operating officer (COO) of a public company to discuss her modern corporate university initiative along with a host of enablement priorities. She was interested in understanding key enablement metrics, benchmarks, and ways to scale knowledge sharing. The COO was looking for feedback and ideas on foundational enablement principles. The company was doing something wrong, as they were missing their revenue bookings targets, their stock was down, and they had tremendous inefficiencies. Teams were doing similar job functions, such as creating organizational charts showing how they would rationalize resources in one model and distribute resources in another. The teams were spinning out of control and were not showing progress on building an enablement strategy for their divisions.

We jumped on a call to discuss where the company was at with their strategy. We listened to their ideas and challenges. What became apparent was that they needed a vision and framework for modern corporate learning, certification, and mentorship. We brainstormed and came up with a "university" concept that would become the foundation for their entire corporate learning culture. I thought that perhaps this was not an isolated example. There must be other companies with similar inefficiencies and needs.

I had a similar conversation with a leader in another public technology company. They had a similar challenge. They asked me how to create a learning culture where every employee is engaged, educated, coached, mentored, and measured. They wanted a way for all employees—from finance and developers to customer support—to have a clear career path from education to promotion. They liked what they saw was happening with their sales teams.

Many companies struggle and need help to build a modern corporate university. A scalable and structured educational program that behaves like a university with curriculum, certifications, community, and learning paths is hard to create and scale. It is not a suitable learning strategy for every company at every stage. You need to be ready. Your culture needs to be ready. Your leadership team needs to be ready. Your employees need to be ready. You need to be ready to make it happen.

The goal of this chapter is to explore how to deliver consistent learning and knowledge sharing inside a larger corporate structure.

When you are faced with similar challenges of scale and silos, consider introducing the idea of a modern corporate university that is made available to everyone. In this chapter, we will answer the following questions: When is the right time to build a university? How do you get teams to rally around the vision? How do you structure a modern corporate university infrastructure? How do you build content for it? How do you get teams to rally around the vision? How do you measure its effectiveness? We will answer these questions with real-life examples of companies succeeding at doing this.

Traditional Learning Doesn't Work

Winning companies have the capability to learn not only faster but also smarter than the competition. They are able to keep up with the strategic developments in their environment as well as stir up the competitive landscape themselves.

The traditional learning management system (LMS) and human resources mindset is not working. LMS is broken for several reasons:

- Learning is considered a chore instead of a value add to employees.

- Learning management systems are not personalized by role and employee.

- Learning is not social and does not enable employees to learn from each other.

- Easy-to-use and engaging content is not easy to find inside corporate walls.

In summary, most corporate learning environments are built around an older corporate LMS that only manages compliance and formal training. Our learning and development teams are spending a lot of their time and resources doing compliance training versus people enablement, resulting in missed goals and undesired outcomes. We are still seeing huge investments, but the return on investment is in question. "The corporate L&D industry is over $140 billion in size, and it crosses over into the $300 billion marketplace for college degrees, professional development, and secondary education around the world."[15]

Selling the Modern Corporate University Concept

Besides the negative sentiment of LMS, the business justification for building a modern university is based on a few factors. First, we want to grow our businesses faster by sharing knowledge and educating our employees. The more they learn and apply, the faster companies will see results. Second, we want to build skills and invest in our people. We want to reduce employee attrition by building skills, demonstrating that we care about our teams' development, and improving employee morale. A well-thought-out, modern educational program sends the right message to employees and is accessible and approachable to learn. We want to help our people fast-track their careers. Third, we want to invest in our corporate culture and build a cost-effective way to scale learning and mentoring.

Remember Q from chapter 2? I interviewed her about her modern corporate learning initiative to see what we could learn from her experiences. Q successfully rolled out a company-wide university learning initiative for all her employees and partners at FinancialForce. Because of her success working with sales, she said the rest of the organization had employee FOMO—fear of missing out. The combination of

---

15 Josh Bersin, "Watch Out Corporate Learning: Here Comes Disruption," Forbes.com, Mar. 28, 2017, https://www.forbes.com/sites/joshbersin/2017/03/28/watch-out-corporate-learning-here-comes-disruption/.

business results, demand, and wanting to make an impact was enough of a driver for Q to take the initiative and run with it. Another reason why the timing was right at FinancialForce to pursue a cross-company corporate learning initiative was that a new CEO and a new chief people officer, also known as a vice president of human resources, joined her company.

The starting point was her success with the sales teams. She created learning paths by role, which included coaching, certifications, self-paced learning, and team-based role plays. As Q started socializing her success and learning paths with the broader organization, light bulbs went on. The teams saw a better way of learning and knowledge sharing. The learning principles were just as relevant for non-sales employees. It helped that the human resources team was hearing great things from salespeople and all the other employees had FOMO.

One thing Q did that was important in her journey was to rebrand the initiative FinancialForce Learning to avoid the objection that it was only for salespeople. A big driver of FinancialForce's modern corporate learning was survey feedback from their non-sales employees wanting education and enablement like the sales teams.

In her words: "We had to run it like a normal sales cycle building a business case and working closely with decision makers and influencers." Q focused her energy on the human resources team. She even joked and said she had to run her own drip campaign like salespeople must do to nurture relationships. She built trust and recognized them as experts in people development, engaging them in a conversation by asking questions like "What am I missing and how is this done today?" Q had to overcome objections, and the non-sales branding was a critical step.

I asked Q why she thought sales was leading the charge. She shared with me that "salespeople like telling stories, and stories are shortcuts to success." Salespeople learn faster through storytelling. They are also competitive people, and their competitive spirit drives change. It is a corporate survival-of-the-fittest reality that we can coin Darwinian enablement. Learning and sharing knowledge is a human-to-human reality. The best sales enablement programs are on the forefront of turning learning into revenue. That is why the modern corporate university is being driven by sales and embraced by human resources.

Another great example of selling the university framework is Amy Pence at Alteryx. Amy understands how to work both top-down and bottom-up in a corporation. She represents her people and also hobnobs with her executives. She shared a story with me about her early days in creating a modern corporate university framework at Alteryx. Amy and I jumped on a call, and she shared with me the feedback she got from Dean, her CEO. His exact words were: "Wow, this is really great to see." Amy shared that Dean thought her modern corporate university plan was well thought out, multidimensional, and inclusive of all groups and departments.

I asked Amy to take me step-by-step through the entire conversation with Dean and her vice president of human resources. She shared that she decided to do a no-slides meeting. She was nervous and remembers distinctively that she took a deep breath before she walked into the room. It was an important meeting. The meeting took place in a small conference room with a round table and a whiteboard. Amy's job was to help the CEO visualize what the future of learning was going to become at Alteryx.

The story started with a review of the success of learning and tools created for sales teams. There was no question that sales enablement was working for the revenue teams. The question became, "What does enablement mean to revenue-generating employees?" Amy led a conversation focused first on Alteryx's value pillars. After going through the entire process and pitch, Dean slammed his hands down on the table, in a good way, and said, "You nailed it." Amy had connected the dots for Dean. Now she has the support of the executive team, which is always the recommended first step in rolling out a modern corporate university.

Amy took Dean through the Alteryx pillars of customers, culture, and communications, which need to work in concert to be aligned and have a meaningful impact on results. The way they work together is by mapping people, product, process, programs, and partners to ongoing learning and new-hire onboarding. The operational rigor is reinforced with key metrics around engagement, retention, net promoter score, employee satisfaction, and productivity. Amy is an excellent example of moving from sales enablement to all-employee enablement. The university framework delivers the center of excellence to make it happen.

Modern Corporate University Framework

The way to start building a university is to create a framework that can be repeatable across roles, levels, divisions, business units, and geographies. The framework will drive learning outcomes consistently by including templates and guidance for knowledge sharing, content structure, coaching, testing, certifications, mentoring, and measuring.

Coming prepared with a framework that is a proven best practice is a great way to get alignment and offers instant credibility. It is also one less thing to do. Once you tailor it to your business and get alignment, you are well on your way to delivering a scalable modern university platform. You should get to a place where everyone in your company adopts your framework and clones for their teams, departments, and roles.

The way to map out a framework is to collaborate with leaders who understand the nuances of the corporate culture and roles. Getting a clear understanding of the curriculum, expectations, and metrics by role make the job of creating a university organized and achievable.

We created the foundation at Salesforce, and we wanted to help many companies at Saleshood. Working with different leaders and cultures put the framework to the test. The companies were chosen because they had explicit internal initiatives led by the CEO to create a university framework. We spent a lot of time understanding the rationale and going deep to understand the problems they wanted to solve and the impacts of solving the problems.

Map Out Roles

In each case, what ended up being a great starting point was a room, a whiteboard, and the enablement leader responsible for pulling together the university framework. What worked well in each situation was to baseline the conversation with roles. The way I do it is to start listing the roles by department. For each role we want to know a few key points, like the name of the leader, top priorities, first thirty-day success metrics, and overall role success metrics. A big success factor is to gain consensus on where to start first. It is important to begin understanding the relative prioritization of the roles and departments.

For each role, we look to create a standardized learning path, including self-paced learning, team-based learning, knowledge checks, certifications, and a resource library. You would share this framework with your stakeholders and start fleshing out a few roles in each area. Begin with sales. Figure 13.1 gives you a visual of the learning path pillars.

Diving deeper into the benefits of scale, now with a broad-based framework, you can focus on detail. Alignment happens because you are providing a framework. You are providing course design templates. You are providing scorecard templates. You are setting certification expectations. You are creating a common language and cadence for learning and knowledge sharing that creates a shared experience and outcomes.

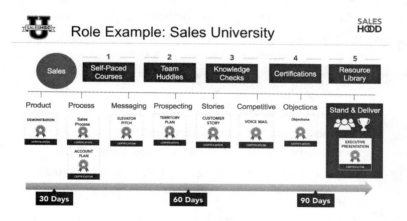

Figure 13.1: Sample Learning Path for Corporate University

Help Departments Tweak Their Content

Give each department and role the autonomy to create their own certifications and curriculum in your framework using their content. With this approach, you help your company scale content creation in addition to content consumption and content assessments. Departments will define their own method of coaching, but rest assured, everyone will want to coach. You must make coaching a big part of your framework. There should be agreement to use a calendar with clear, distributed ownership of the timelines and schedules.

> "Organizations need to retool learning,
> changing it from an obsession on individually focused
> and content-driven events to learning that is deeply
> contextual, social, and embedded into real work."[16]

Another great benefit of a modern corporate university framework is making promotions and career planning more open and transparent. Making the learning path by role and by department available for everyone to review and discuss in performance reviews and one-on-ones is a great way to drive up employee morale and people development.

Do all of this and you become the person providing the template to drive scale. Your reputation becomes one of a corporate learning enablement profession. You become known as the person who solved one of the most challenging company problems of scale and learning. I bet when you pull this off,

---

16 Todd Warner, "Corporate Learning Programs Need to Consider Context, Not Just Skills," *Harvard Business Review*, Nov. 10, 2017, https://hbr.org/2017/11/corporate-learning-programs-need-to-consider-context-not-just-skills.

you will be called up onstage by your CEO and recognized as executive of the year just like Marc Benioff recognized me at Salesforce.

Best Practices to Creating a Modern Corporate University

After working with many companies to flesh out their university framework, here are nine best practices that every university leader should be thinking about before embarking on the journey.

Get Top-Down Support

It's imperative to get the company's top executives or top management—all the way up to the CEO—behind the new-forming enablement organization to demonstrate commitment and focus. Selling this internally is hard. One of the most important goals is to ensure that the project has support from the CEO down. Alignment is key.

Craft a Vision Statement

With top executive support, I recommend that you document a vision statement and a strategic plan of the corporate university. Words matter. Answering the "why" is critical to employee engagement.

Secure Resources

You must then build a realistic budget and a funding strategy that includes content development and resource allocation. Building a university is expensive.

Define Roles

Then you should determine the prioritization of the audience or stakeholders who will use the corporate university. Building out a role-based plan by department is the way to create consistency and personalization.

Create Learning Paths and Templates

The organization must determine how the needs of the audience will be met while continually pursuing the strategic goal of the corporate university. Do this by completing the learning path by role.

You should then develop a university template for how products and services will be designed to consistently achieve goals. The template should include detail about course design, team workshops, knowledge checks, certifications, and resources. Expectations around content development should be standardized across university participants. Scale is the key here.

Involve Stakeholders

Curriculum and created content should go through a development review process. Create a program management office where all stakeholders agree on timelines and content delivery assumptions.

Ensure Accessibility

The use of technology and resources to be used by the corporate university must be determined. It is important to ensure the university is accessible anywhere. Mobile and video are both expected as standard.

Monitor Goals

Metrics and accreditation should be developed that will allow the organization to continually monitor its progress against the university's strategic goals.

Communicate

Communicate the vision of the corporate university constantly and consistently. A big theme of this book is the importance of communications in driving change and our initiatives. It is no surprise we need to do it with the modern corporate university.

KEY TAKEAWAYS

The modern corporate university is a strategic imperative you should consider when the timing is right for your company. Look at the maturity of your organization and go-to-market and gauge when the timing is right to pursue.

- You know you are ready when you have too many teams creating content and curriculum in an unstructured and inconsistent way.
- Look for clues like lower employee productivity, poor results, bad product launches, too many silos, and the same content and curriculum being created over and over.
- Being recognized as the champion of your modern corporate university is a great professional legacy.
- Take your time and get it right.

Build your skills and mindset to be an enablement professional and multiplier. Be the enabler that creates an enablement culture. You decide how these pieces fit together and how and when they come to life in your company journey and professional career.

Because you have dedicated your career to bring out the best in everyone else, this book was dedicated to you to help bring out the best in you! We are living through a global movement and rise of the enablement profession. Embrace it. Enablement starts with you being enabled and being the best you can be. Rise up to the challenge and let's do this together.

Acknowledgments

The idea for this book emerged during a brainstorming session with Chris Do and Ben Burns. We were talking about the SalesHood brand in Santa Monica, California. It became apparent to me that we were not doing a great job with making our brand communication strategy speak directly to enablement professionals. Chris and Ben pushed me to focus on enablement professionals in our marketing, and I walked away from that daylong discussion inspired. Once I had that clarity, I knew I needed to write my second book for every past, present, and future enablement professional on the planet. Thank you Chris and Ben.

I want to thank the SalesHood investors and advisors who believe in and support all the work we do at SalesHood. Without you, we would not be able create the stories that fueled this book. Arjun Gupta and Lindsey Armstrong, thank you for being our chief believers.

I want to thank all the contributors of stories and experiences to *Enablement Mastery*. You are the crazy ones. You partner with us every day to help our teams be the best they can be. Thank you to Amy Pence, Quyen Chang, Sheevaun Thatcher, Linda Page, Jake Hofwegen, Dan Dal Degan, AJ Gandhi, Mark Siciliano, Nick Sarles, Bob Kruzner, Laurie Schrager, Chris Messatesta, Roque Versace, Chris

Harrington, Kelly Frey, Kamal Ahluwallia, Aaron Farley, Neil Hudspith, John Hsieh, Barry Rhein, Amy Itaya, Bruce Campbell, Matt Cameron, and Blair Crump. Thank you to my friend and mentor Jim Steele for writing the foreword of this book and for always being the executive who steps up and leads by example.

Enablement Mastery would not be possible without the support and commitment of the team at SalesHood. I want to give a special thank you to Dave Lichtman, Tait Henricksen, Victor Nguyen, Deb Scherba, Ira Bernstein, David Lam, and Aileen Ho for working so hard to raise awareness of enablement and make enablement adopted more and more as an industry best practice. I'd like to also thank Josh Cruickshank for coming up with the name of the book in one of your practice elevator pitches. Thank you to Barry Rhein for the ongoing coaching, mentorship, and love. I want to thank my cofounder, partner, friend, and brother Arthur for always being available and for the never-ending support. Hood on three, everyone.

I want to share gratitude to my family for giving me the inspiration to keep writing every day. Thanks to my parents, Etty and Maurice, and my sisters, Rita and Tammy. Thanks to Jenn for enabling me to keep writing, and thanks to our kids for teaching me new things every day.

With gratitude,
Elay

Index

About the Author

Elay Cohen is the CEO and cofounder of SalesHood. He is the former senior vice president of sales productivity at Salesforce. Elay was recognized as the "2011 Top Executive" by Marc Benioff and credited for creating and executing all of Salesforce's sales training and coaching programs that accelerated its growth from a 500 million-dollar business to an enterprise worth more than 3 billion dollars. The innovative sales training and support delivered over these years by Elay's team to thousands of sales professionals resulted in unprecedented hypergrowth.

Elay authored the book *SalesHood: How Winning Sales Managers Inspire Sales Teams To Succeed*. Elay is a thought leader in the discipline of sales management and is sought after by the most successful CEOs. He is also recognized as a top innovative "Mover and Shaker" in sales leadership by *Entrepreneur* magazine and also recognized by LinkedIn as one of the world's top sales experts.

Elay is on a mission to improve and modernize how companies enable their people. Elay is working closely with the world's most innovative companies and most forward thinking educational institutions. Together, they are changing the future of work.

About the Author

Elay Cohen is the CEO and cofounder of SalesHood. He is the former senior vice president of sales productivity at Salesforce. Elay was recognized as the "2011 Top Executive" by Marc Benioff and credited for creating and executing all of Salesforce's sales training and coaching programs that accelerated its growth from a 500 million-dollar business to an enterprise worth more than 3 billion dollars. The innovative sales training and support delivered over these years by Elay's team to thousands of sales professionals resulted in unprecedented hypergrowth.

Elay authored the book *SalesHood: How Winning Sales Managers Inspire Sales Teams To Succeed.* Elay is a thought leader in the discipline of sales management and is sought after by the most successful CEOs. He is also recognized as a top innovative "Mover and Shaker" in sales leadership by *Entrepreneur* magazine and also recognized by LinkedIn as one of the world's top sales experts.

Elay is on a mission to improve and modernize how companies enable their people. Elay is working closely with the world's most innovative companies and most forward thinking educational institutions. Together, they are changing the future of work.